D1474820

RAS
105.5
F2
76m
00

Medicalized Motherhood

13/02

Medicalized Motherhood

Perspectives from the Lives of African-American and Jewish Women

JACQUELYN S. LITT

RUTGERS UNIVERSITY PRESS
New Brunswick, New Jersey, and London

Library of Congress Cataloging-in-Publication Data

Litt, Jacquelyn S., 1958–
    Medicalized motherhood : perspectives from the lives of African-American and Jewish women / Jacquelyn S. Litt.
      p. cm.
    Includes bibliographical references and index.
    ISBN 0–8135–2781–3 (cloth : alk. paper). —ISBN 0–8135–2782–1 (pbk. : alk. paper)
    1. Motherhood—United States. 2. Child care—United States. 3. Maternal health services—Social aspects—United States. 4. Child health services—Social aspects—United States. 5. Jewish women—Pennsylvania—Philadelphia Interviews. 6. Afro-American women—Pennsylvania—Philadelphia Interviews. I. Title.
HQ759.L57 2000
306.874'3—dc21
                                         99–43560
                                           CIP

British Cataloging-in-Publication data for this book is available from the British Library

Portions of this book previously appeared, in different form, in the following publications:
"Pediatrics and the Development of Middle-Class Motherhood," *Research in the Sociology of Heath Care* 10 (1993). Reprinted by permission of JAI Press.
"Mothering, Medicalization, and Jewish Identity," *Gender & Society* 10, no. 2 (1996). Reprinted by permission of Sage Publications.
"American Medicine and Divided Motherhood: Three Case Studies from the 1930s and 1940s," *The Sociological Quarterly* 38, no. 2 (Spring 1997). © 1997 by The Midwest Sociological Society.

Manufactured in the United States of America

For Jim and Elliot
and
My parents, Mona and Leonard Litt

Contents

Acknowledgments

The owner and chef at a local Middle Eastern restaurant asked me whether I could taste the difference in her falafel since she returned from Israel. She explained that she had gone to Israel to refine her cooking, and that the lessons and interactions she participated in laid the groundwork for her improved techniques. "You can't make a falafel alone" was how she summed it up.

I didn't write this book alone. *Medicalized Motherhood* emerged from many interactions and lessons I have enjoyed while doing this work. My deep appreciation goes to the women who agreed to participate in this study, who took the project seriously and spent a great deal of time on it. I stayed in touch with many of them while I continued to live in Philadelphia, and was fortunate to have been invited into their lives with such openness and warmth. These are remarkable women, who show us strength, humor, and intelligence as they negotiate the contingencies of their everyday lives. I thank Alison Hirschel for helping me locate many of the respondents.

A community of feminist scholars has nurtured me along with this book. Barbara Katz Rothman, Judith Gerson, Leslie Bloom, and Modupe Labode generously read the entire manuscript and provided crucial comments and direction during a pivotal stage in the writing. Each of them emphasized a different point of interpretation, and challenged me about issues I thought I had already settled. I profoundly thank them for helping me make this a stronger book. Maureen McNeil is my collaborator on another project on motherhood discourse. Working together has deepened my understanding of how mothers' care work is structured and negotiated through expert systems of surveillance. I greatly appreciate her comments on this manuscript, which she engaged and critiqued through the years with characteristic brilliance. Emily Abel also played a major role during the writing of this book, reading the manuscript numerous times, and identifying areas where I needed to sharpen my conceptual and historical focus. Her incisive reflections and magnificent readings vastly improved this book.

Craig Hosay, Lynne Litt, Jane McCafferty, Diane Eyer, Cornelia Flora, Sherry Wellman, David Miller, Cindy Anderson, Christine Bowditch, Carole Browner, Cheryl Gilkes, Kathi Conger, Ellen Gray, Gloria Jones Johnson, Susan Watkins, and Elizabeth Higginbotham offered critical commentary and reactions through the interviewing and analysis phases of the research. Their willingness to listen and reflect added considerably to the argument I subsequently developed, and made the everyday work of interviewing and writing a little less intimidating.

Iowa State University provided me with essential support for writing the book. Willis Goudy, chair of the sociology department, and Jill Bystydzienski, director of women's studies, gave me resources and time to complete the manuscript. A Faculty Development Grant from the College of Liberal Arts and Sciences provided financial support for the final stages of research. Rand Conger offered me a home at the Institute for Social and Behavioral Research to complete the manuscript. And Maren Sand, my undergraduate research assistant for the last three years, gave to the project her remarkable skills and support. I thank her for her many hours of work on my behalf.

Judy Gerson, David Mechanic, Alan Horowitz, Patricia Roos, Katherine Jones, and Gloria Cook generously welcomed me to Rutgers University, New Brunswick, in women's studies and sociology and at the Institute for Health, Health Care Policy, and Aging Research while I was preparing for and conducting the interviews. Joan Ravel did much of the transcribing, and I am indebted to her skill and commitment. Rutgers was an exciting place for conducting this research and through my experience there I learned a great deal about feminist theory and health issues.

Working with Rutgers University Press was equally as rewarding. Martha Heller, the acquisitions editor, offered exceptional advice and conversation in redrafting the manuscript. David Myers, Marilyn Campbell, and Susannah Driver-Barstow were wonderful to work with during the production phase and provided much support in crafting a better book.

The project was funded largely by an Officer's Discretionary Grant from the William T. Grant Foundation of New York City. Dr. Robert Haggerty, president of the foundation, and I spent hours discussing the historical trajectory of pediatrics and its implications for mothers. I am grateful for these conversations and for the funding to carry out this project.

I want to extend my gratitude to my sister, Lynne, to my brother, Jonny, to my sister-in-law, Renee, to my aunt Gloria Aks, and to my parents, for their loving support of and interest in my work. And to Rosie, for reasons we know. To my husband, Jim McGlew, for generously reading, rereading, and re-rereading this manuscript, for offering breathtaking insights, essential editing, and nudges along the way to expedite the process, and for helping me to forge the life I always wanted, I offer my deepest thanks and love. And to our son, Elliot, who made me a mother, I owe more than words can say. While not making this book a speedier one to write, he certainly has made it more meaningful.

Medicalized Motherhood

Introduction

In the early 1940s Donald Geddes, an editor at Pocket Books, approached the pediatrician Dr. Benjamin Spock and asked him to write a book for parents on child care. According to Spock, Geddes told him, "The book we want doesn't really have to be very good, because we are only going to charge a quarter and can sell ten thousand copies a year easily" (Spock and Morgan 1989:132). *Baby and Child Care*, of course, far exceeded its publisher's expectations; Spock's book sold 750,000 copies in 1946, its first year of publication, and by the early 1970s it had gone through two editions and over 200 printings, and achieved total sales of more than two million (Zuckerman 1975). Spock's manual, still in print in 1999, is the most widely used baby book in U.S. history.

While we cannot know precisely how women in the 1940s approached the new guidelines for mothering outlined in Spock's manual, we can say with certainty that the book's soaring popularity was rooted in the ethic of "scientific motherhood," a cultural product of the nineteenth and early twentieth centuries. From women's letters, diaries, and medical case reports, it appears that most American women in the first half of this century were exposed to the modern ideas of child care contained in experts' texts. What mothers believed about these expert ideas, how they used them in daily practice, and how they affected their conceptions of mothering are the subject of this book.

Medicalized Motherhood addresses scientific motherhood from the standpoint of women (Smith 1987); in other words, from the perspectives of women who were the intended audience of expert knowledge. The data in the book come from oral history interviews I conducted with eighteen Jewish and twenty African-American women who raised their children in the 1930s and 1940s. The book also draws on my extensive review of the published medical writing in pediatrics during these decades (Litt 1993) and on seven interviews with physicians who practiced in these years.

The mothers that I interviewed, like most in the 1930s and 1940s, saw themselves as primarily responsible for child care in their households. It was in this context of maternal responsibility that the women forged their relations to dominant medical discourse on motherhood and child care. Yet what differentiated these women from many others is that as ethnoracial minorities[1]—as Jews and African Americans—their mothering was treated by white public health officials, medical experts, and social reformers with a good deal of mistrust and skepticism. Because of the marginal place they occupied in the dominant picture of American motherhood, the Jewish and African-American women's relationships to medical discourse differed from those of Protestant, white, middle-class women for whom inclusion in the category of "good mother" was not contested along ethnoracial or class lines. Scientific motherhood, like motherhood in general, was a social and cultural space "occupied by groups of unequal power" (Collins 1998:5). Women varied in their standing in this divided motherhood, and "gain[ed] or los[t] identities as outsiders-within by their placement in these social locations" (5). Collins describes the contradictions of living in an "outsider-within" position. "Under conditions of social injustice, the outsider-within location describes a particular knowledge/power relationship, one of gaining knowledge about or of a dominant group without gaining the full power accorded to members of that group" (6). I argue that it was Jewish and African-American mothers' negotiations of their "outsider-within" position that provided the groundwork for the cultures of motherhood they developed.

The notion that middle-class domesticity (i.e. whiteness, marriage, and women's dependence on wage-earning men) is the crucial feature of acceptable motherhood has roots in the colonial idea of "Republican motherhood" (Kerber 1995). The bifurcation between "good" and "bad" mothers continued into the period in which the women in my sample grew up and then raised their children; white mothering experts either condemned some women's mothering practices as undeserving of intervention, as in the case of African-American women, or they targeted mothers as objects of regulation and assimilation, as in the case of Jews.

The narratives of the African-American and Jewish mothers I interviewed reflect these ethnoracial and gendered notions of motherhood. The narratives are steeped in quandaries about the women's own social position. Mothers read medical discourse as promoting a gendered and racialized respectability, not simply as a set of technical requirements for their children's good health. Like other cultural artifacts that represented modernity and acceptability for women in the first half of the twentieth century, such as the new beauty culture (Peiss 1998), the slender body (Brumberg 1997), and "American" feeding practices (Shapiro 1986), medical principles of motherhood were similarly racialized, and were understood by the women I interviewed as linked to the dominant, acceptable form for motherhood.

Women related to medical discourse as a normative system, as a kind of gateway between the "old-fashioned" and the "modern." They did so together with other women who were much like themselves. Despite medicine's promise to link them in a common, virtuous motherhood, mothers related to medical discourse in ways that activated ethnoracial and social class divisions among women.

A word about the analytic framework is necessary here. As a study of women's narratives, this book presents a close reading of what women have to say about their mothering, in particular how they portray the link between their motherhood and ethnoracial and class status. The ethnoracial identities the women describe were structured by the ethnoracial assignments given to their groups. Thus, my analysis of their narratives explores the relationship between their mothering ideas and identities and the wider ethnoracial assignment of Jews and African Americans. Ethnoracial assignments were promulgated in popular and scientific literature as well as institutionalized in legal, political, and medical codes. These were socially constructed categories that took on meaning in relation to particular meanings of ethnorace in the first third of the twentieth century (Brodkin 1998; Frankenberg 1993; Omi and Winant 1994).

By examining how Jewish and African-American women took up the new medical commands about motherhood, we gain a historical perspective on how the ethnoracial system has affected the development of medical expertise in motherhood. *Medicalized Motherhood* argues that rather than being a site where women claimed a source of commonality with other women, scientific motherhood was constituted as a site of heightened ethnoracial and class differentiation among women. As their material resources, status needs, and social networks differed, so did the ways these women took up the dominant medical discourse on mothering. But beyond identifying simple differences in their approaches to expertise, this book also shows how the social relations of scientific motherhood involved women in socially segregating practices. Scientific motherhood, as these women were involved in it, positioned all women as caretakers of children yet simultaneously differentiated them along ethnoracial and social-class lines.

Medicalization, Scientific Motherhood, and Women's Lives

Medicalization, as it has been conceptualized, is a social process that has developed since the end of the nineteenth century involving issues central to both men's and women's lives. Medicalization is the process through which medical interpretations of conditions have acquired cultural legitimacy, eclipsing other perspectives toward human problems and conditions such as religious and moral frameworks. Through the twentieth century, the domain of medicine has expanded to include mothering practice as well as childbirth, old age, death, child growth and development, alchoholism, behavioral problems, sexuality, attention span, anxiety, appearance, and eating problems as requiring the intervention of medical experts. Medicalization involves legal and economic institutional structures in its support. Through cultural and institutional practices, medical understandings have become the dominant frame for understanding a large range of personal and social activities and have come to undergird modern systems of social control and belief. Sociologists examine the mechanisms and implications of applying the medical model to this widening array of human problems (Conrad 1992; Freidson 1970; Litt and McNeil 1997; Reissman 1989; Rothman 1998; Zola 1994).

Changes in the practices and meanings of childbirth provide an excellent example of how medical authority and power expand. Prior to the twentieth century, virtually all women gave birth at home, in a setting that was controlled and defined by women midwives, kin, and neighbors who attended to the birthing women. By 1950, almost 90 percent of women gave birth in hospitals, the result of a process that had largely given the role of midwives and women's networks to male obstetricians (Leavitt 1986). The meaning of pregnancy changed too; it was (and still is) largely treated as a disease, requiring specialized medical intervention that professionals control. The history of childbirth points to the complex and contradictory nature of medicalization. Much feminist scholarship has examined the health dangers and women's loss of power and control over childbirth (Ehrenreich and English 1979; Oakley 1984). Much recent scholarship focuses on the medical as well as social hazards for women raised by the new reproductive technologies (e.g., in vitro fertilization) and argues that the earlier medicalization of childbirth paved the way for the current medicalization of reproduction (Carson 1994; Franklin 1997; Franklin and Ragoné 1998; Martin 1992; Rothman 1986, 1989). The current surveillance that pregnant women undergo regarding smoking, alcohol use, caffeine intake, et cetera, is similarly understood as a dimension of the medicalization of reproduction and yet another lever for the medical as well as social control of women (Humphries 1999; Litt and McNeil 1997). A few scholars emphasize the racialized implications of medicalized childbirth (Fraser 1998; Lee 1996; Logan 1989).

"Scientific motherhood," the expanding jurisdiction of medical experts over sick as well as healthy children, followed a historical trajectory similar to that of reproduction and childbirth. A debate among scholars about the costs—and to a lesser extent, the benefits—of the medicalization of mothering has also emerged (Abel 1995, 1996, 1998; Apple 1987, 1995).[2] Scientific motherhood was a contradictory discourse. As a new system for the regulation and evaluation of mothering practice, it was designed to extend accountability but not autonomy to mothers. In her review of the history of scientific motherhood, Rima

Apple shows that it limited women's control over child rearing, making women "both responsible for their families and incapable of that responsibility" (1995:162). While medicine and science offer modern societies authoritative parameters through which mothers' practices are defined and evaluated, we still know remarkably little about what this has meant for women or, more to the point, for ethnoracial and class divisions among them.

It is my intention in this book to examine this contradiction of motherhood from the perspectives of women whose ethnoracial positions made their maternity the object of suspicion. Was scientific motherhood a new, scientifically justified means by which minority women were rendered submissive to white male medical authority? What, if any, resources did scientific motherhood offer to women in controlling their own households? Their relations to men? And what are the implications of this ideology for relations among women of different ethnoracial and class positions? My interest lies in locating not just women's agency—how they garnered some autonomy through this regulatory discourse—but in how women brought medical discourse into being as a gendered project of ethnoracial and class identity. I focus, then, on how mothers organize their representations of scientific motherhood along ethnoracial and class lines, and how through their practices of scientific motherhood they engage and produce relations of difference and identity with other women. I argue that women cultivated various motherhood cultures, some more and some less oriented toward medical discourse. But beyond that, I show that women used medical discourse not only as a system of technical knowledge to improve child health but also as a site for negotiating their relations to other mothers both within and outside their ethnoracial and class groups.

Valerie Lee (1996) argues that a bias toward white women has informed the feminist scholarship on medicalization. In her research on the "granny" midwife tradition among African Americans, Lee found little scholarship on the kinds of midwifery practiced in black communities. It has been African-American women writers (such as Alice Walker, Toni Cade Bambara, Gloria Naylor, and Toni Morrison) who have recovered the missing knowledge of African-American "granny" midwives: "Feminist social scientists have reclaimed nurse midwifery [whereas] it has been left to African-American women novelists to preserve the language, lore, and learning of the grannies" (1996:24). For Lee, the history of modern medicine has been a history not only of gender conflict but of racial and class conflict as well. The fate of African-American women's racial struggles and the history of medical power are, in Lee's view, inextricably intertwined.[3] In her groundbreaking treatment of medicalization as a gendered as well as a racialized enterprise, Gertrude Fraser amplifies Lee's point: "Motivations for the insertion of medical authority in the bodies of women differed radically depending on the implied and explicit objectives of the polity and on the social construction of race" (1998:126). Lee and Fraser point to the history of medicalization as a site where white power has been institutionalized and given scientific authority. *Medicalized Motherhood* highlights the distinct importance that medical discourse has played in how women themselves use class and ethnoracial differences to construct motherhood.

The Women

The thirty-eight women I interviewed were born between the years 1894 and 1930, and all but seven had their first child in the 1930s or 1940s. All of the Jewish women were married in the years they raised their children, and the nine who worked outside the home did so in family businesses (see appendix). Fifteen of the eighteen Jewish women are the daughters of Russian immigrants and three are migrants from Russia. We shall see that their status as upwardly mobile first- or second-generation immigrants played a large role in shaping Jewish women's relations to medical discourse.

The African-American women were more diverse in their social-class position than the Jewish women. Two women raised their children with the help of upper-middle-class resources and networks; some of the others were stable working class; some were working poor. Their marital and employment status also varied (see appendix). Eleven of the African-American women were married when they raised their children and four of these were employed. Two of these four worked as domestics. Nine of the African-American women raised their children as single mothers. These were the poorest women in the sample. All of the single mothers worked for wages, and seven worked in some service or domestic capacity.

Taking Care of Baby: The Gendered Division of Labor

The married women—Jewish and African American—believed that women and men held different responsibilities for housework and child care. Phyllis Taylor,[4] an African-American woman, explains that her husband's help around the house "was unheard of . . . In that time he worked and, uh, brought the money home. And all the child rearing was left to me, just about. He was there on weekends and all." Sylvia Epstein, a Jewish mother, states "it was a rough time because my husband never touched a child. This was a mother's, you know, that's your job." And Sadie Horowitz, a Jewish woman, explains how she saw the division of parenting responsibility:

> Well . . . he worked. He put in a lot of hours at Curt Manage-
> ment. But he was helpful. Sometimes he would even take turns,
> you know. We would sterilize the bottles, so he'd wash the
> bottles and sterilize them. Sometimes make the formula, you
> know, while I was doing something else. No, he was very
> helpful.

Women took it upon themselves to carry out and organize most of the housework and child care. Consider the situation of Edna Levin, a Jewish woman I interviewed, who deemed it her responsibility to do the child care work. What this meant, she said, was an obligation to protect her husband from it. She characterizes her domestic work life as oriented toward "pacifying everybody." On the one hand, she worked in the luncheonette her parents owned:

> I mean, it wasn't a place where you had a lot of extra help. And
> at lunchtime everybody would run in from the factories.
> Everybody would run in at the same time. My brother was
> working. My sister was in school, I think. So I was the only one
> around. . . . So, more or less, you know, you feel sorry for your
> mother, so you try to help. So that's why I would help my
> mother in the business.

On the other hand, Edna took full responsibility for her household and child care. After working in the luncheonette, Edna fed and bathed her child. Then she got the house ready for her husband's return at dinnertime.

Edna believed that she was responsible for protecting her husband from the pressure, noise, and work of child care:

> He would go to the food distribution center to buy merchandise [at 4:00 A.M.] so, you know, you want to make it calm for your husband [when he got home from work]. So that was it. I wouldn't want him to have a crying baby around or whatever. . . . I don't say I was right doing it that way, because he should have been able to take care of her, too, and all that. But I tried to save him from that.

When I asked Edna why she thinks now it might not have been right, she replied:

> I think maybe I should have left her up. Her father would have been able to take care of her more. But I figured being the man [he] gets up so early in the morning, he shouldn't have to do that. . . . I don't know that he fed her too often. I don't really know that he fed her. I think I always had it done before he got home. He was very chicken, anyway, when it came to her. Ah, and he was giving her a bottle for me. I don't know what I was doing at the time. And accidentally, he dropped it. The bottle slipped out of his hand. He didn't actually hurt her nose. The kid didn't even cry, I don't think. But he got so upset about it that I thought he was gonna pass out. Then one time, he did something else and he did pass [out]. He went in bed and passed out. He banged her head. And, uh, next thing I know, he was in the bed. That was it. [I told him] "It was an accident. She's okay." What would it do to hit him with it? What? That's why I said if I had given him more time with her, that wouldn't have upset him as badly as it did. But, um, I was crazy, I guess, because I thought this was the better way to do it.

All of her friends "were sort of the same way":

> My one girlfriend that I am very close with, she was the same way with her kids and her husband. We always tried to shield 'em. Like my husband when he would come home, I never asked him to put out trash. He never shoveled. He never washed his car. He didn't even know how to put storm windows in because I was under the impression . . . the man works hard.

He gets up early. Why should he have to come home and do these things? So I would try to shield him from all this. Wasn't the wisest thing to do. I was the one that did it all. But, uh, this was my theory.

Edna refers to her responsibility in straightforward terms, assuring me that she wasn't forced but chose to organize her child care and housework in ways that met the diverse needs of multiple family members. She took great pride in being able to juggle these various responsibilities. Yet it was deference to her husband's (putative) needs that provided the structure of her daily routine and her definition of motherhood.

In her study of women's household work, Sarah Berk (1985) argues that negotiations such as these around housework are central to how women enact their accountability to gendered norms. Household work, she argues, has two outcomes: the production of goods (meals, clean laundry, etc.) *and* the production of gender. The gender-typed household represents an interactional achievement, producing a division of work that assigns child care to women and protects men from it. At the same time, this division of work is an arena where women and men negotiate their gender identity and position.

Gender was also negotiated by the women in my study around the question of whether they would seek paid work. Mothers' employment represents what Lamphere labels a "cultural problematic" (1993:183), a tension between the dominant ideology, which places mothers at home full time, and the realities of markets, wages, and the desired standard of living. When I explained to one mother on the phone during our first conversation about the interviews that I wanted to talk to her about mothering issues, she declared, "Oh, I don't know much about that. I worked." In interview after interview, women stated that their husbands preferred them to forgo work and stay home full time, often with the justification that this was best for the children. These narratives reveal how, for the married mothers in this sample, obedience to husbands and full-time motherhood were clearly linked, while paid work and motherhood were mutually exclusive.

Celia McNeil, an African-American woman, discusses paid employment in terms set by her husband:

> When I met [my husband] I was working off and on. I worked
> in a factory. I worked as a trimmer. And he was in debt and I
> helped him get out of debt and when he did I did all the work
> around the house. He made good money. . . . I didn't have to
> work. And he was the first black driver [for the company]. And
> he made foreman. Yeah, he made foreman. So, he was getting a
> nice salary. I didn't have to work . . . like most black women.

But Celia's rationales were even more complex. She described her
husband's considerable pressure on her to stop work:

> He didn't want me to work. Well, I did go to work a couple of
> times. I just got bored [at home], like after the children got a
> certain [age]. . . . What was I gonna do after I finished what I
> had to do? So I got a little, I always got a part-time job. And it
> would always be something in the evening . . . and he would
> brainwash me until I stopped. I always quit. . . . He said I had
> enough to do staying here taking care of the children.

Celia reveals that being a good wife in this context was to support and
enact her husband's conception that he could provide for the family.
Part of this was justified and explained as necessary for the children.

The organization of child care in single African-American mothers' households reveals a different kind of gender order from what we
find in married women's households. Living without a partner freed
women from what Marjorie DeVault calls the "force of male preference"
(1991:148). On the other hand, without the benefits of a man's wage
these women were much more likely to be poor, even though all worked
for wages. And all of the nine single mothers developed extensive and indispensable relationships with women's networks extending beyond the
mother-child unit and relied on these networks for everyday help in
raising their children. We shall see that these networks played a large
role in securing women's distance from medical discourse.

Given this gender order of women's responsibility for children, it
is no surprise that the world of child care and the relations to medical
discourse the mothers describe was one largely controlled by women.
Rarely did I hear of a situation where a male relative or friend (except
for a physician) intervened in the everyday health care of children. Seen

as a matter of women's responsibility and as a symbol of womanhood, caring for children and negotiating medical norms of motherhood took place primarily within a women's world.

Method

I conducted the interviews during 1991 and 1992. All the interviewees resided in Philadelphia, Pennsylvania at the time of the interview. The interviews took place through a brief preliminary conversation and more extensive conversations during the following weeks. These lasted from one and one-half hours to four hours each. I interviewed each woman in her own home. Each interview was tape recorded and transcribed. When possible, I mailed the transcribed copy of the interview to the respondent. I also interviewed seven physicians who practiced during that time.

I solicited volunteers for my interviews from a number of social service agencies, senior citizen community centers, and apartment complexes. I gave presentations at a number of Jewish Community Centers, where I met most of the Jewish women I interviewed. My networks among the African-American women were more diverse. Some I met through African-American professionals in the city who recommended friends and families. Others I met through a legal aid office, where some of these women were seeking legal help. And others I met through a conventional "snowball sample" in which one volunteer would recommend another friend or acquaintance.

In my interviews with the mothers I used semistructured interviews (Reinharz 1992), thematically focused on medical and child care issues. I asked women questions about how they viewed and used medical experts in their child care practices. I emphasized four general areas: their own childhood relations to and awareness of physicians, their experiences as young mothers dealing with health and medical issues concerning their children, their daily activities surrounding infant and child health, and their reflections on the meanings of modern medicine for their mothering. My main challenge was to encourage women to talk about the meaning of medicalization, a project that I saw as related to gender issues but not, I thought at the time, to ethnoracial ones. During the interviews I asked mothers what it meant "to take" or "not to take" their children to a physician. Not surprisingly, these were diffi-cult questions for the women to answer; "the meaning" was not some-thing they had ever articulated. At the time, I was unsure what I wanted to hear. But I did have a sense that to understand women's medicalized cultures I needed to know how they took medical discourse home with them.

My interest in how medicalization intersected with the production of ethnoracial and social class inequality came midstream in the inter-view stage of my project, and largely as a product of reflecting on the ups and downs of the interview process itself. My initial interest in medicalization was to assess empirically the important feminist theo-retical issue of women's relationship to expert knowledge and its link to gender inequality (Benjamin 1993; Code 1991; Collins 1990; Goldberger et al. 1996; Harding 1986, 1993). What happened to moth-erhood, I wondered, when it fell under the regulation and measurement of medical professionals? Adrienne Rich's (1976) distinction between the experience and institution of mothering seemed particularly apt: if motherhood could be structured without the patriarchal regulations such as those found in medicalized mothering, it could be both emotionally and politically empowering for women in ways it is not currently (Chira 1994; Eyer 1993). My reading of the sociology of professions, the his-tory of medicalization, and feminist theory had alerted me to the patri-archal assumptions that were embedded in scientific ideas about women but not fully to how the fractures among women along ethnoracial and class lines would be instantiated in the medicalization project itself. These fractures, I came to understand, had multiple and often unan-ticipated consequences for gender inequality.

It was through my interactions with the women I interviewed that I came to see medicalization as a process that both reflected and fueled powerful ethnoracial and social-class divisions among women. An early set of interviews revealed to me that my project on medicalization would need to address these matters. The women whose practices were medicalized spoke to me as if we had much in common—as if the faith in modern medicine and the desire to become modern mothers were taken for granted, commonly accepted, and understood. This was par-ticularly true of my interviews with Jewish women, who, as a group, were remarkably similar in their orientations toward medicalization.

Elsie Reisner's remark captures the common view: "I don't know about today, but in this area that we're talking about doctors were idolized and looked upon as gods. You know? If you didn't trust your doctor, you didn't trust anybody." Because these attitudes were closest to those I had grown up with as a middle-class Jewish woman, our conversations were familiar: we talked about the importance of physicians and of science, we spoke some Yiddish (which established me in the interviews as Jewish), and we joked about the home remedies their own mothers had used. In the taken-for-granted features of the interviews, medicalization appeared gendered—it was women's responsibility to carry out—but not rooted in ethnoracial factors.

It can be a great advantage in interview contexts for women to interview other women; some modes of communication are presumed and established (Oakley 1981). But this commonality is increasingly understood to obscure as much as it enlightens, and feminist discussions also focus on how ethnoracial and/or class differences between researcher and respondent affect the interview, analysis, and publication process (Bloom 1998; Gluck and Patai 1991).[5] Indeed, because of my feelings of affinity with the Jewish women's perspectives I was especially blinded to the normative race, ethnic, and class power that medicalization contained.

For the women who evaluated medical discourse more critically, largely the African-American women, I came to see that my questions and my presence positioned them in a context of evaluation that highlighted our differences. It was in these moments of tension (or what might be technically called "probing") that I was able to see how medicalization held meaning in racialized and class terms—and that my questions and my very presence in their homes represented divisions along these lines. Here I began to see how I epitomized and borrowed the discursive power of medical discourse. Some of the less medicalized women seemed to become defensive when I asked them to explain why they had not consulted a physician regularly in raising their children or why they continued to use the home remedies they did. Their defensiveness was a result, in part, of my status as a middle-class, educated white woman in the context of a study on medicalization. It is not insignificant in this context to raise the lamentable history of racism in the established medical profession. In essence, I represented the very culture whose meanings I was asking women to scrutinize.

This took me some time to see. My status as white and middle class, as benefitting from racial privilege and power, was clear to me as I began this project; but what that meant for my association with medicalized, professional culture I had failed to see. For all my interest in "meaning," I remained unaware, for far longer than I like to admit, that for women whose practices were not medicalized, my persistence in asking them about their practices served as an implicit critique of their established practices as mothers.

Yet another insight developed during these interviews: how my own critiques of medicalization as a regulatory discourse on motherhood were embedded in perspectives of women with access to medicine. Reading scholarship about poor African-American women's situation in the current U.S. medical system (Abraham 1993), reading about the history of black health activism in the U.S. (Smith 1995),[6] and interviewing a number of African-American physicians and health activists made me acutely aware that medicalization held different meanings for people of different social-class and ethnoracial positions. Most particularly, I came to see that the medicalization of birth and child care was something only the privileged could afford to reject. Since the Progressive Era, African-American health activists, women and men, have fought for access to the expanding medical sphere and for the elimination of the racism that was institutionalized in medical practice. Access to good care signaled the difference between African Americans' survival or destruction. The early work of Booker T. Washington's Tuskegee health projects, Negro Health Week campaigns, and the black women's club and church movements of the first half of the twentieth century, testifies to the central place that improved access to medical care has held in movements for racial equality. While I saw that women's exclusion from mainstream medicine created cultures of resistance against the hegemony of medicalization, I learned also not to romanticize this marginality (hooks 1990).

I have chosen to highlight these dilemmas in my discussion of method because I think it is vital to situate my position as researcher/writer in relation to the research process. Mothers' care of children held tremendous significance in the period under study: mothers' practices were seen to signal the difference between child health and illness and, equally as important, between the production of worthy as opposed to unworthy citizens. Ethnoracial differences between mothers structured these debates, where only some women, primarily white, even held the possibility of becoming "good" mothers as defined by the cultural imperatives of white dominant society. Given the accentuated cultural emphasis on motherhood, the reflections I encouraged women to make about their own maternal practices, and my own social position as a white, Jewish, professional woman, some women I interviewed must have felt the need to fashion their narratives in defense of their own actions.

In her analysis of storytelling, Pam Carter suggests that women's facility at telling stories (in her case, breast-feeding stories) stems from their defensiveness. Because of the inordinate attention given to women's mothering activities, women "need to have a story at the ready to defend themselves against possible criticism, to explain themselves as a mother and a woman" (1995:200). Embedded in the narratives that Carter examines are descriptions of women asserting themselves against and within the terms of the dominant motherhood discourse, although the forms of assertion that mothers used varied greatly. Tess Cosslett, in her study of fictional accounts of childbirth, concurs. She argues that women construct narratives as "negotiation[s] with official discourse . . . [to find] ways to cast themselves as significant characters in their own birth stories" (1994:155). In my study, sometimes women's attempts to "cast themselves as significant characters" meant invoking medical norms and thus their acceptability; other times, it meant an erasure of their own agency and thus their distance and protection from blame; still other times their mothering was invoked as necessity, not choice, again distancing the women from blame and rendering them acceptable. Mothers very much geared their narratives toward constructing themselves as good mothers. It was within this context of contending with dominant discourse that the mothers I interviewed created their narratives, and in so doing, their affirmations as mothers. It may be that this need to "polish up their stories" emerged and took on particular meaning in the context of the interview situation itself, where I represented the normative, professional discourse.

Thus, women's stories are not objective accounts of their mothering practice. They contain much more than narrations of activity; they reveal intersections between the present and the past, one of which is the interview process itself, and reflections on their own lives in relation to the dominant normative constructions they perceive as relating to child care, then and now. In this way, women's narratives can be seen as narrations of self and social position (Bloom 1998);[7] the narrative data represent the activities of mothers but also their attitudes about the normative meanings of motherhood. I am less interested, then, in documenting the actual practices that mothers describe (although there is some of that in the following chapters) than in considering the meanings of motherhood that women constructed in the course of the interviews themselves.

Outline of the Book

The next chapter, chapter 1, provides the reader with a historical background on scientific motherhood and the conceptual approach that *Medicalized Motherhood* takes to it. Thereafter, the book is divided into two parts. Part I, "Encountering Medicine, Constructing Motherhood" examines women's narratives of encountering scientific motherhood. It focuses particularly on the meanings these women gave to medicine as an approach to baby care that separated them from their own parents. And because these women identified medicine in the context of their changing social position, these chapters consider explicitly how the context of migrancy and social mobility affected mothers' discourse of medicalized mothering.

Chapter 2 examines how the Jewish mothers mobilized medicalized mothering practices to signify their advancement from their parents' immigrant culture into the American middle class. Mothers portray themselves as benefiting from the new opportunities of American freedoms, as actively seeking self-improvement, and as engaging medicine in the context of their changing group membership. Chapter 3 focuses on the narratives of the African-American women who migrated to Philadelphia from the South and for whom migration generated their first encounters with modern medicine. Yet rather than perceiving themselves as participants in the new momentum of progress, the working-class

migrant women positioned themselves as separate from the social world
that medical discourse represented, viewing their relation to this new
world of modernity as distant and tentative. What all of the women
have in common, Jew and African American, is that they constructed
medical discourse as a site of dominance and measured their relation
to it as a sign of their own social inclusion.

The narratives tell us much about how women view their identity,
position, and ambition. The different quality of their narratives, the
openness and optimism of the upwardly mobile Jewish women and the
longing and nostalgia of the working-class African Americans, can be
situated within the different structural opportunities for social mobility that these women encountered. Benmayor's assertion that the func-
tions of storytelling vary in diverse contexts of mobility speaks to this
point:

> For Puerto Ricans, telling life stories is not a process of passing
> down treasured family lore or the experiences of the past to
> later generations who no longer share the same class position as
> their immigrant forebears. The "rags to riches" stories of many
> older European immigrants are predicated not only on indi-
> vidual achievement but on the collective upward mobility and
> social access enjoyed by those groups as a whole. . . . For young
> Puerto Ricans today . . . the stories of their parents and grand-
> parents who eked out a modest living as factory or domestic
> workers contain strong and painful parallels with the present.
> They have strategic, immediate value, giving historical perspec-
> tive to current struggles, drawing out connections between the
> oppressive conditions, then and now. (1987:3)

As we shall see, much of how these women constructed their new encounters with medical discourse—their unfolding relation to modernity
and social divisions—had to do with their understandings of the "op-
pressive conditions" of their past, "then and now."

Part II, "Women's Networks, Divided Motherhood, and the Legiti-
mation of Medical Authority," foregrounds the place of women's networks in their relation to medical discourse. Chapter 4 examines how
Jewish women's networks facilitated their embrace of and access to
medicalized mothering. Surrounded by other Jewish women with similar social ambitions and household resources, these women engaged

medical practitioners with the consent and support of their closest peers. Furthermore, the Jewish women consulted primarily Jewish physicians, not a distant medical establishment. Immersion in networks of other Jews was how these Jewish women organized and understood their relation to medical discourse. Chapter 5 examines a parallel structure among a small number of upper-middle-class African-American families. It identifies a highly consolidated and well-established network of African-American professionals that supported women's medicalization. Again, it was not as strangers but as guided insiders that these African-American women found their way to developing a medicalized culture of mothering. In Chapter 6 we find a very different picture of women's networks' relations to medicine. Here we examine the poor and working-class African-American mothers, who had only marginal ties to medicine.

In these chapters we find the importance of an individual's immersion in a social context for the production of health beliefs and practices (Freidson 1970; Pescosolido 1992). But beyond that, I argue in these chapters that women's ties to their networks produced a socially segregating culture around medicalization. Women forged their relations to medicine in ways that articulated, even intensified, ethnoracial and class divisions among women that were already in place. It was in the context of these segregated cultures of mothering that medicalization acquired its meaning as a symbol for motherhood.

Chapter 1   Scientific Motherhood

The new attention the medical establishment paid to child care grew out of the social movement of scientific motherhood, which dates to Catharine Beecher's *Treatise on Domestic Economy*, published in final revised form in 1842. "Scientific motherhood" refers to the idea that mothering should be guided by scientific supervision and principles (Apple 1995). The ideology of scientific motherhood solidified in the Progressive period, as child-rearing experts began to acquire greater legitimacy and as federal and state programs, such as publicly funded maternal education and infant welfare clinics, came to support child-rearing experts' view that scientific knowledge could (and should) be applied to household practices (Ladd-Taylor 1986).[1]

The new science of motherhood was a component of the broader cultural change in which science was understood to improve virtually all facets of life, from worker productivity to reproductive control (LaFollette 1990).[2] This shift involved an epistemological transformation—what Paul Starr characterizes as "the retreat of private judgment": "The less one could believe one's own eyes—and the new world of science continually prompted that feeling—the more receptive one became to seeing the world through the eyes of those who claimed specialized, technological knowledge" (1982:18). Popular magazines of the period such as *Scientific American* promulgated this view, communicating the developments and complexity of science; they celebrated, for example, the "men of science" who "peered out at the world." In these magazines scientists were said to have distinctive "brainpower" and "stamina" and were described with masculinized metaphors of activity and strength drawn from their laboratories, such as "coiled springs" and "gas under pressure" (LaFollette 1990:69–70). Nonscientists (i.e. all women and the majority of white and non-white men) were portrayed in these popular cultural materials as passive observers and admirers who waited to see what "science would do for society" (76).

Mothers were the special target of the campaign to popularize science and, as managers of households, were seen by experts and reformers as pivotal to the project of modernization (Apple 1987, 1995).[3] Women's magazines, advertisements, government pamphlets, visiting nurses, home economists, and mothers' classes all conveyed the necessity of scientific training for housekeeping, feeding, and baby care. One writer for a home science magazine warned mothers to "equip themselves for motherhood as thoughtfully, conscientiously, and zealously as any other scientist prepares himself for an exacting career" (quoted in Apple 1995:166). Mothers too perceived the need for this guidance; in some years as many as a hundred thousand women wrote letters to the U.S. Children's Bureau for advice on raising their children. One estimate is that over one-half of all women received some professional advice during the decades around the turn of the twentieth century (Ladd-Taylor 1986). Elevating homemaking and mothering to the status of a professional career did not, however, promise mothers autonomy over their own practices. Rather, as motherhood came to be seen as dependent on science, mothers were portrayed as incapable of performing child care without expert guidance.

What fueled this radical change in the dominant social approach to motherhood? How did centuries of motherhood practice, rooted historically in religion, community custom, and self-reliance come to be understood as inferior, as expendable in relation to the scientific? For an answer it is necessary to look first at the health concerns that dominated at the turn of the century. Besides the children's diseases with which we are familiar today, such as chicken pox, measles, and mumps, children faced the potentially fatal diseases of diphtheria, scarlatina, smallpox, whooping cough, tuberculosis, infantile paralysis, and influenza. Infant mortality rates were also extremely high and garnered a great deal of attention from the medical and public health reform communities. Lowering infant mortality was a difficult task, as it addressed the intersection between biological and social conditions. Then, as now, infant mortality rates varied dramatically along socioeconomic and ethnoracial lines: poor and immigrant infants, most of whom lived in poor tenement districts in eastern cities (New York, Boston, and Philadelphia) were more vulnerable to death within the first year of life than infants in higher social classes, as were poor African Americans and whites living in the South (Hagood 1939; Meckel 1990).

As serious and terrifying as these health conditions were, however, it was not only death and disease that fueled the Progressive period's ideology of scientific motherhood. White elites found in the ideology of scientific motherhood a response to gender, racial, ethnic, and class conflicts of the late nineteenth and early twentieth centuries, particularly those animosities wrought by immigration, industrialization, and urbanization. Scientific motherhood was held out as offering a new scientific basis for promoting social stability in the midst of these radical social upheavals, for reinscribing, above all, the traditional gender order, cultural homogeneity, and white dominance.

Scientific Motherhood and the Ethnoracial Divide

According to Karen Brodkin (1998), the massive waves of migration from southern and eastern Europe (which included Russian Jews) beginning in the late nineteenth century fueled new racial assignments for Europeans; northern and western European immigrants earlier in the century assimilated easily to American customs and citizenship—they were treated essentially as white. By contrast, late-nineteenth-century immigrants from southern and eastern Europe were considered, in Brodkin's words, "not-quite-white" (1998:56). These new migrants were associated with communism and labor unrest, lived in segregated communities, and were concentrated in certain occupations—factors that marked them as racially distinct from whites, not-quite-black but not-quite-white either. By occupying this ethnoracial middle ground, these immigrants became the object of a great deal of political, scientific, and social regulation.

An 1889 medical article by Dr. Abraham Jacobi, known as the

"father of pediatrics," highlights the "civilizing" role that science should play in "amalgamating . . . the scum of all the inferior races":

> If there is a country in the world with a great destiny and grave responsibility, it is ours. Its self-assumed destiny [is] to raise humanitarian and social development to a higher plane by amalgamating, humanizing, and civilizing the scum of all the inferior races and nationalities which are congregating under the folds of our flag. Unless the education and training of the young is carried on according to the principles of sound and scientific physical and mental hygiene, neither the aim of our political institutions will be reached nor the United States fulfil its true manifest destiny. (quoted in Halpern 1988:53)

In Jacobi's view, as in that of other physicians and scientists of his day, "scientific physical and mental hygiene" held the solution to this "civilizing" mission of the United States (Kraut 1994).

In the second decade of the twentieth century the theories of eugenics—selective breeding for a "better" (i.e., whiter) humanity—represented a hardening of the rhetoric around racial assignment. The Galton Society, established by Charles Davenport in 1918, for example, promoted eugenics and lobbied for limits on immigration. In addressing the "white nativist anxiety" (Brodkin 1998:95), the eugenics movement tied together gender, race, and women's biology (Collins 1999; Kraut 1994). By 1924, immigration from Asia had become virtually impossible and, from Europe, increasingly difficult.

Tying motherhood to racial assignment held particular promise as an ideology of ethnoracial regulation. The animosity that elites directed toward the new "not-quite-white" Europeans was gendered: ethnoracial minority women were criticized for pooling economic and social resources with other families, taking on paid employment, using traditional remedies, and organizing political movements—in short, they were "bad mothers" who deviated from middle-class norms of domesticity. One observer of attitudes in 1912 put it this way: "Women from Poland, Lithuania, Russia, southern Italy, and Syria were increasingly associated with ignorance, backwardness, and low evolutionary development and frequently portrayed as 'loose women, poor housekeepers, and bad mothers'" (quoted in Brodkin 1998:94–95).

Fears about reductions in white native women's reproduction were generated by this "anxiety" about declining white dominance. In this context, white government officials, scientists, and reformers incited popular fears about white "race suicide," proclaiming that nonwhites were outbreeding native whites. Theodore Roosevelt proclaimed that good mothers are "sacred" but the (white) woman "who shirks her duty, as wife and mother, earns the right to our contempt" (quoted in Ladd-Taylor and Umansky 1998:10). Compulsory sterilization laws for a range of putative deficiencies (such as "feeblemindedness" and alcohol abuse) were passed in many states; women of color and these off-white Europeans were the primary targets. Hence, in this new science, ethnorace and gender combined to create a new category of the good and worthy mother against the bad and unworthy one (Brodkin 1998).

It was not only the white male leaders of the public health and medical establishments who linked motherhood to race, but also the white women involved in the Progressive Era reform movement known as maternalism. In the years between the world wars, these reformers (largely of white northern European stock), supported social policies to counteract the effects of "ignorance" on poor mothers and children and solve the so-called political dilemmas of a racially diversifying Anglo-American social order. Despite ideological variation, maternalists shared the view that motherhood was organized in ethnoracial terms (Ladd-Taylor 1994; Mink 1995). Yet rather than view racial characteristics as fixed, as the racial hereditarians of the eugenics schools believed, maternalists believed in the promise of assimilation and staked their legislative and neighborhood intervention on it. These reformers portrayed motherhood as women's special calling and as a unifying force for women—in other words, as the answer to the racial divide.

Reform campaigns were designed to improve mothers' status in the home and in the public domain; in effect, to transform minority women into fit Americans. They fought for mothers' pensions and the elimination of child labor and developed mothers' classes and infant-welfare clinics. Some were also instrumental in the passage of the first federal infant-welfare act, the Sheppard-Towner Act, in 1921, which, among other things, tightened legislation around midwives and funded baby clinics (Ladd-Taylor 1986).

Here too science was used to racialize notions of motherhood.

White maternalist reformers directed their efforts toward "protecting immigrant children" and "modernizing immigrant families" and used the tenets of scientific motherhood to do so (Ladd-Taylor 1994:5).[4] Urban immigrants received messages about the benefits of American customs from many sources; immigrant newspapers, insurance bulletins, mainstream newspapers, as well as physicians and nurses. It is particularly relevant for the understanding of scientific motherhood that the reform of the domestic unit and of women's everyday practices were among the most important targets of change, as historian Elizabeth Ewen explains: "The tension between immigrant women and the representatives of industrial culture was not over the need to change the external conditions of motherhood in an urban slum environment, but over how and what knowledge was to be incorporated into the rhythm and pattern of daily life" (1985:139).

Modern medicine's usefulness for "family health" was a mainstay of Americanization campaigns. In schools, immigrant children were taught about modern precepts for cleanliness and health, with the hopes that they in turn would instruct their parents. One settlement project, the influential Hull-House in Chicago, set a national model for immigrant education, declaring immigrants' child-rearing methods and child-feeding habits "peculiar," "improper," and unsanitary in the American context. A director of New York City's milk stations (where pasteurized milk was distributed) described his impression of the backwardness of these mothers in a way that was typical in this movement:

> The Italian mother who ties a string of coral beads around her badly-fed baby's wrist to make him get red blood . . . the Polish mother who packs her baby's soiled clothes in the bottom of a tub, sets him on them, and sozzles him with this water, from the bath; the Jewish mother who tries the formula that saved Mrs. Bobscheffsky's child on her own child—to its extinction—all require infinite patience and reconstruction. (quoted in Meckel 1990:131)

Gwendolyn Mink argues that this reform effort "individualized the burden of maternity and infancy protection, hanging the infant's welfare on the assimilation and education of the mother" (1995:72). In doing so, white maternalists insisted that even these so-called "inferior" races could be taught to conform and therefore challenged the belief in the immutability of biological racial traits (the hallmark of eugenic thought). Yet they also promulgated the contention that "inferiority and inequality inhered in cultural difference" (Mink 1995:72).

However demeaning this view of "not-quite white" mothers, Polish, Jewish, and Italian women were treated as having the potential for assimilation. African-American women, men, and families, by contrast, were considered beyond the scope of most white Progressive-era reform efforts (Mink 1995). While white maternalist reform promised to unite women in a common motherhood, black women were considered unworthy objects of maternal education and assimilation, beyond salvaging as mothers. According to Collins (1999) African Americans symbolized the essence of the primitive and superstitious against which science defined its modernity and superiority. "Racial reasoning" was embedded in the constructions of scientific advance: "Rather than viewing modernity as a passive backdrop for the development of the natural, physical, behavioral, and social sciences, scientific professions helped manufacture and legitimate notions of modernity through a racialized and gendered production of scientific knowledge" (Collins 1999:275). African-American women faced a scientific and reform establishment that viewed them as objects of study and control rather than improvement and assimilation.

Eugenic and other scientific racism positioned African Americans at the extreme end of the evolutionary trajectory, claiming that blacks had "pathological psychology" as well as "biological inferiority" (Fraser 1998:102–103). African-American women were represented in popular culture (art, films, school texts, medical literature) as immoral and sexually promiscuous. A 1904 newspaper article about the problem of immorality among "Negroes" written by a white woman exemplifies this racist approach: "Negro women evidence more nearly the popular idea of total depravity than the men do. . . . When a man's mother, wife and daughters are all immoral women, there is no room in his fallen nature for the aspiration of honor and virtue. . . . *I cannot imagine such a creation as a virtuous black woman* (emphasis added; quoted in Higginbotham 1993:190). Because of the "racial reasoning" embedded in notions of science and motherhood, African-American women were considered off-limits by the white reform establishment. Beyond that, the segregation of African Americans in schooling, housing, health care, and jobs limited women's social mobility as well as their access to new advances of science and medicine. Those women who received some guidance were offered instruction in paid domestic service, but not support for their own mothering. Moreover, the geographic isolation of most African Americans in the South at this time left them without the cultural reform offered by maternalist projects, from early schooling to vocational programs, including mothering (Fraser 1998).

In northern cities, white maternalists did not address the poverty and racism faced by African-American women until the New Deal years. Mink identifies the exclusionary strategy that decades of discrimination and segregation implied: "Pegging equality to cultural conformity while withholding the tools and the choice of conformity from African Americans, liberal racism [contained in maternalist reforms] marked the Black mother, worker, and child as unassimilable" (1995:120). By being excluded from the possibility of assimilation, African-American mothers were denied a share in the modernization project. Gertrude Fraser explains how African-American mothers were positioned as permanent outsiders to the promises of scientific motherhood:

> Even with the best maternal and infant care, whites assumed that African Americans would retain what they had defined as inferior traits. For them, it would be impossible for a "Negro" really to participate in American society, except in the narrow boundaries that had been reserved for him or her. In the case of maternal and infant health care, African Americans received few of the idealized rewards of scientific progress and permanently lost much of that which had helped to sustain them. (1998:127)

As applied to African Americans, scientific motherhood was not a sign or mechanism for manufacturing social inclusion; as the Tuskegee syphilis experiments revealed, African-American men (and by implication women and children) were viewed as objects upon which scientific medicine could be tested, not as persons worthy of treatment and improved health (Brandt 1978). Historian Judith Leavitt's (1986) study of childbirth practices in the United States documents how white middle-class women in the early twentieth century began to demand the new medical technologies that male birth attendants controlled. The poorest women, African Americans among them, were actually the most vulnerable to these new medical practitioners, who used them as bodies to practice on. The most and least privileged women were the first to experience medicalized childbirth, but they did so under radically different circumstances.

It is important here to highlight that as African Americans in the South and North were not considered full citizens, federal and state legislation effectively stripped local black communities of their own infrastructure of health care. In her case study of the decline of African-American midwifery in the South, Fraser (1998) argues that the new regulations on black midwives cost black communities a great deal. While the decline of white midwives also created pressures on white women to medicalize their childbirth, many white women could be seen as trading up; because of their access to medical care, many were promised physical well-being at the same time as they were congratulated for completing their maternal responsibility to produce "pure" white children.

Most African-American women made a different trade. Involvement in medicalized rationales did not assure them of better health care (for it was often worse than that provided by midwives and local healers), nor did it necessarily guarantee social acceptability, in large part because public health services were themselves stigmatized. As Fraser writes, woven into the South's public health service and the enlarging control of African-American midwives "was a language of shame, stigma, and pollution keyed to racial difference" (1998:103). And while African Americans did turn to this stigmatized public health service, they received, along with medical attention, "damaging cultural narratives" (104) about their biological inferiority and maternal inadequacy.

Thus, the promise that scientific motherhood could serve as the lever to the "rewards of social progress" was a promise held out only to those who could and did "whiten" in the dominant racial classification. African Americans, in the racial taxonomy that was reproduced and fueled by scientific racism, were considered permanently nonwhite (i.e., permanently inferior). They formed the symbolic opposition against which "whites" defined their insider position (Brodkin 1998). Where Jews occupied a racial middle ground which was whitened after World

War II, African Americans positioned as social "others" could not even begin to benefit from their claims to social justice until the civil rights reforms of the 1950s and 1960s.

Whatever maternal education and support African-American mothers received came largely from other black women. Reform work among African-American women took place in churches, clubs, settlement projects, and among midwives (Fraser 1998; Higginbotham 1993). African-American maternalists had a relation to maternal education and uplift that differed from that of the white maternalists: they viewed the domestic ideal as a promise to offer them—as well as their working-class and poor counterparts—respectability in and resistance against dominant culture. Higginbotham elaborates the "politics of respectability" that was developed by African-American Baptist women reformers in the Progressive Era, reformers whose strategies for racial uplift followed many of the principles of white maternalists but did so in a context of opposing racism. Church women advocated that African Americans adopt the "manners and morals" of the white dominant society, not to position themselves as subservient to whites, but rather "as a highly self-conscious concession to hegemonic values" (193):

> By claiming respectability through manners and morals, poor black women boldly asserted the will and agency to define themselves outside the parameters of prevailing racist discourses. Notwithstanding the sincerity of the Baptist women's appeals to respectable behavior, such appeals were also explicit rejections of Social Darwinist explanations of blacks' biological inferiority to whites. Respectability was perceived as a weapon against such assumptions, since it was used to expose race relations as socially constructed rather than derived by evolutionary law or divine judgment. (1993:192)

The politics of respectability offered the possibility of challenging years of social injustice. African-American church women "believed respectability to be the first step in their communication with white America" (Higginbotham 1993:916). These politics were expressed directly through personal behaviors, as a 1915 document of the Baptist Women's Convention proclaimed: "Fight segregation through the courts as an unlawful act? Yes. But fight it with soap and water, hoes, spades, shovels and paint, to remove any reasonable excuse for it, is the fight that will win" (quoted in Higginbotham 1993:193). Higginbotham's emphasis on the resistance contained in the politics of respect shows us how black church women used assimilation—what we might call scientific motherhood—as a strategy to both expose and contest racist representations. The goal, according to Higginbotham, "was to distance oneself as far as possible from images perpetuated by racist stereotypes" (196).

This rhetoric linked the everyday activities of mothering to the wider system of ethnoracial classification. African Americans' respectability required that every individual take responsibility for self-regulation and improvement—to "fight segregation . . . with soap." The engineers of racial uplift used the dominant culture's emphasis on motherhood as a mechanism for racial equality, arguing that the mundane matters of child feeding, hygiene practice, housekeeping, dress, and so on were deeply significant for the fight against racism and segregation. Beyond that, these women argued publicly and forcefully that nurturing African-American children and communities was a valid and important goal in its own right, a view not shared by the dominant white society. African-American women's project of modernizing motherhood, then, represented an even more radical act than did the Jewish women's modernizing efforts, for it challenged the dominant racial taxonomy, the basis for racial assignment, and white society's neglect of African-American children.

Well-Baby Care: The New Middle-Class Focus of Scientific Motherhood

By the 1930s the institutional apparatus of maternal education had moved to professional medicine, particularly pediatrics and obstetrics. Advice manuals targeted maternalist reformers as themselves problematic, and warned women that it was only physicians who were qualified to make the distinction between the superstitious and the scientific (Litt 1993).[5] Childbirth practices took on a decidedly medical cast too. And so with mothers' feeding practices; between 1920 and 1950 more and more mothers reported that their children's feeding was under a physician's care (Apple 1987). Increasingly, women's magazines advocated, according to one historian, the importance of "follow[ing] specialists' directions without necessarily understanding them" (Leavitt 1986:175).

At the same time, a new division between the services for wealthy/ middle-class and poor mothers was institutionalized in health policy and the organization of medical practice, a division that in some ways paralleled maternalist and public health reform. The distinction between public and private services intensified after 1928 when Congress repealed the Sheppard-Towner Act. The number of publicly funded child health centers established in urban centers dropped from a high of 429 in the period between 1920 and 1924 to 32 in 1930 (Halpern 1988). At the same time, these clinics (which were refunded through the 1935 Social Security Act) imposed new income restrictions which excluded mothers with middle-class incomes, effectively dividing mothers who could afford a private physician from those who continued to qualify for public clinic services. Vanished were hopes that maternal and child health would function as an entitlement for women of all social classes. Instead the state now supplied medical treatment only to disadvantaged and needy families, solidifying the division between private and public health care systems (Fraser 1998; Ladd-Taylor 1994; Meckel 1990).

What happened in the new private medical office that more and more white middle-class women consulted? How was the normative model for good mothering now defined? By the 1930s, the medical emphasis had shifted to managing the activities of healthy infants and children. Childhood diseases—many associated with poverty—became less common and infant mortality declined. Infectious disease rates dropped. And many of the earlier life-threatening infectious diseases were controlled with the new antimicrobial sulfa drugs in the late 1930s and penicillin therapy in the middle 1940s. The predominant medical thinking about child health care then moved away from these life threatening conditions to more middle-class concerns, which involved feeding, vaccinations, normal growth and development, and "well-baby care"—in other words, ways to care for essentially healthy children (Halpern 1988).

From the late 1920s on, according to some medical estimates, well-child care constituted one-third to one-half of all visits to physicians— and mothers in the United States consulted physicians in record numbers (Apple 1987).[6] Sydney Halpern describes this medical approach as revolutionary: "Never before had practicing professionals concerned themselves in a systematic manner with the normal growth and development of individual children" (1988:88). A major pediatric figure of the time, Dr. Gordon Veeder, distinguished the new physician's role as a "counselor of health" from the earlier focus on disease: "Child hygiene is at present the most important motif in our work, as it will continue to be in the future, and in child hygiene work it has been the child that has been the topic of consideration—not disease or medicine. . . . The change in conception of the physician from the healer of disease to the counselor of health is the great advance made by the present era of medicine" (quoted in Halpern 1988:96). Another pediatrician elaborates the importance of the household to child health. In an article published in *Archives of Pediatrics*, Dr. Joseph H. Marcus compels his colleagues to "bring up" parents (read: mothers) to become good caretakers: "We cannot depend on the school or the church to train the child. We must rely upon the parents, who must be taught how to handle their children from both a physical and psychological standpoint. Who is going to teach them? The physician must to a certain extent. The pediatrist is face to face with this problem. It is his responsibility to advise and 'bring up' the parents" (Marcus 1925:455).

This focus required a spotlight on households, particularly mothers' practices within them. "To examine a child without an opportunity of making acquaintance with the mother is to be deprived of evidence which may prove essential for correct [medical] judgment" warned Dr. Hector Charles Cameron (1921:199). Medical "therapy" was directed toward teaching mothers "about their own shortcomings," warned Dr. R. S. Miles (1921:667). Recognizing that "mothers are sure that any such criticism is a personal insult" (Huenekens 1925:21), pediatric journals counseled physicians about how to cope with this delicate situation. Dr. Garry C. Meyers explains: "Pediatricians must not discourage the mother by blaming her errors for the child's faulty habits, but must tactfully correct her mistakes in a constructive way. This should be done at the time of prophylactic consultation with the mother in a receptive mood rather than on the occasion of an illness which has already disturbed her mental balance" (1929:676).

This ethic of well-baby care brought mothers' routine activities under medical surveillance and secured the tie between mothers' work in the household and children's health needs. The ideal mother made routine medical visits. And in orienting mothering toward medical standards, mothers were warned to shift away from their own standards of evaluation to ones that gave authority to the observations made by experts. A 1935 Metropolitan Life Insurance booklet on child care shown to me by a woman I interviewed warned mothers that they must rethink, if not reject, their own perceptions of infant needs: "Measuring the degree of illness of a baby by observation of the symptoms is not always easy for the widely experienced person. So it is no wonder that parents are often puzzled and worried over the question of whether to call the doctor. Here let us remind you is one of the most important reasons for having a regular checkup."

The checkup—a new feature of medical practice—was designed to assess and monitor infants' and children's development; infants were weighed and measured and mothers were interviewed about feeding practices and their daily routines. Physicians offered feeding recommendations and training (habit) management. These visits were supposed to take place weekly during the early months, and monthly until one year of age; through age three, mothers were supposed to take their children in every three months (Halpern 1988). One physician reported in *Hygeia*, the American Medical Association's popular family health magazine, that the road to better child health was being paved by parents' use of "regular physical check-ups" for their children. "We have a good start [on lowering childhood morbidity and mortality] . . . as a large percentage of parents are educated to the idea; many of them are only too glad to pay a reasonable fee for the health protection thus afforded their children" (Gengenbach 1936:1080). There is an irony that this warning comes in the midst of the Great Depression. Dr. Gengenbach makes it appear as if ("fatherly") medical monitoring—and by implication respectable motherhood—is within the reach of each and every mother, if only she would set proper priorities.

Medical assumptions about mothers' purported ignorance and potential danger might have led physicians to question prevailing domestic and parenting ideals that place children squarely in private, domestic units cared for by women. At times medical models did just that. When children were seen to be stuck in bad habits or resistant to parents' training, physicians sometimes recommended that the child be moved to a relative's home or to an institution for a time to generate new, healthier habits (Abel 1996). But the major impetus in medical writing was on reforming motherhood and toward establishing a family and household environment that was oriented toward medicalized child health. In setting this orientation, medical writing intensified the importance of the mother; it naturalized the gender-based division of labor in households and the sanctity of households for child care.

By the 1940s, then, we see the erosion of an essentially nonprofessional system of child-care expertise and its replacement with one controlled in medical terms by medical practitioners in a medical context. In that shift, science came to be understood as less understandable by mothers and as requiring translation by formally trained professionals. Beyond that, the shift signaled a movement away from women-centered institutions (such as settlement projects) to ones controlled by men, typically white and middle class. In the years between 1880 and 1930 the medical profession emerged in its modern form, with formal associations, specialized training, licensing boards, and a widened cultural authority. This also gave medical institutions power over other approaches to health and child care. More and more life activities, from birth to death, were shifted to hospitalized settings. As experts and formal institutions of medicine gained legitimacy as the primary location and source of knowledge about mothering, understanding of mothering changed. Experts increasingly pitted themselves against mothers, a conflict that continues into the late twentieth century (Kaplan 1994; Litt and McNeil 1997; Markens et al. 1997; Rapp 1990; Rothman 1989). Medical authority was increasingly solidified while mothers' lack of compliance with medical regimes came to be seen as a sign of maternal neglect, even abuse (Abel 1998; Gordon 1994; Tsing 1990).

Conceptual Approach

This book follows a conceptual model of the study of scientific motherhood that emphasizes "intersectionality" (Collins 1999), which I use in two ways. The first examines scientific motherhood from women's perspectives, as the intersection between medical discourse and its uses (Clarke and Olesen 1999). I consider what medical discourse and medicalized mothering look like in women's daily lives. The second highlights how ethnoracial and social-class differences and inequality among women figure into the production of mothers' medicalized cultures. Taken together, these two approaches treat medicalized motherhood as a creation of women's agency and a site for the production of gender, ethnoracial, and class inequality.

EVERYDAY LIFE AND MEDICAL DISCOURSE

*At present we remain so profoundly ignorant of how
ordinary people in the past have actually regarded health
and sickness, and managed their encounters with medical
men, that our initial priority should be to "defamiliarize"
ourselves with the assumptions of modern physician-
focused history and sociology of medicine, and hack our
way into the empirical forests of the past in all their
strangeness and diversity.*

Roy Porter

Roy Porter (1985:176) argues for the importance of the everyday, or what he calls the client's or "sufferer's" perspective, for social studies of medicine. Porter's observation about medical sociology and history is particularly apt for our study of women's relation to medical discourse. Most scholarship has focused on how medicalization has developed in and through the formal institutions of medical care and has generally excluded women's caretaking work in households in considering these developments (Abel 1995; Glazer 1993; Litt 1990). There are many reasons for this sociological blinker: the historical tie between the medical establishment and medical sociology, the division of academic labor between anthropologists who study "indigenous" cultures and sociologists who study "modern" ones, and the failure to see women's work in households as health-related labor, as even relevant to the medical sociology enterprise.

This means that the study of women's health-related labor in their households has received less attention than the health-related labor of physicians, nurses, aides, and other such workers (Glazer 1993). As more and more of the health care performed in families moved to formal medical settings in the first half of the twentieth century, many scholars have presumed that women's health-related responsibilities went with it. Yet although the family's relation to formal systems of health care has changed with the development of modern medicine, women were not relieved of their caregiving responsibilities but gained new ones, as Emily Abel explains:

> Family care-giving is not a timeless and static endeavor, changing only through the gradual loss of its medical component. Nor does an hour of professional care translate directly into an hour of relief for family members. Rather than assuming that families withdrew their services . . . we should ask how the revolution in medical knowledge and practice transformed the content and meaning of the care that continued to be delivered at home. (1995:478)

It has been primarily feminist studies that have drawn attention to the production and meaning of science in everyday life—and to the explicitly gendered nature of this history. Much recent feminist scholarship examines the intersection between science and the social relations of reproduction, and identifies this intersection as a key site where gender, sexuality, and kinship are produced in contemporary culture (Franklin and Ragoné 1998).[7] Another line of feminist scholarship focuses specifically on scientific motherhood, on the convergence between medicine and the regulatory discourses of everyday mothering (Abel 1995, 1996, 1998).[8] This research elaborates the conditions under which women themselves have demanded and resisted the medicalization of their daily mothering activities and draws attention to the significant role that women have played in the history of medicalization as consumers, advocates, and experts in scientific medicine. By looking at science as women produce it in their everyday lives, this scholarship problematizes the dominant narrative of women's role as passive witnesses to the march of science; in particular, women become agents in the process of medicalization.

A focus on women's everyday practices in households points to the pivotal place that women have held in the development of modern medicine's expanding cultural authority and institutional power in the first half of the twentieth century. As caretakers in their households and communities and, as we shall see, agents in social-class mobility, women stood in the central position of deciding what the new medical discourse of child care would have to do with their own mothering practices: without mothers' embrace of medical frameworks, medicine could not have gained the authority in mothering and in child care it came to possess. Of course, medicalization also changed motherhood. Through their work for families, women confronted, evaluated, and made novel meanings of motherhood out of the new, medicalized properties of daily life.

The analysis of the everyday shifts the focus away from formal medical institutions and texts to the negotiated meanings and uses of expert discourse in everyday life. Accordingly, this approach sees that scientific discourse is produced, legitimated, and contested in places beyond the medical text, medical institution, or scientific laboratory: museum displays, back-porch conversations, corporate board rooms, medical waiting rooms, science fairs, and kitchen tables are places where medicine's meaning is generated, as much as in the operating or medical examining rooms. Lay individuals are scientific practitioners of their own sort; they are not formally trained and paid to "do science," but they confront science in multiple sites and carry out their lives in relation to it. Methodologically, this has meant generating new ethnographic work on women's negotiation of science in various settings, identifying and studying women's writings (diaries, letters, etc.), and conducting interviews with women, replacing the prevailing tendency to focus on the published writing of medical men and the formal histories of medical institutions (Clarke and Olesen 1999).[9] To use this approach, in other words, is to study science and medicine "on the street" (Martin 1994a:64).

Medical discourse does not function simply as a set of textual directives to which women are rendered passive and by which they are objectified. Dorothy Smith provides a standpoint approach for analyzing textual discourse that integrates women's practice with patterns of social stratification. She refers to textual discourse as occupying a "ubiquitous point of reference" for dominant forms of femininity (including mothering), holding all women responsible despite the plethora of circumstances in which they live (1990:175). Feminist analysis of this "point of reference" involves searching for contested and multiple meanings women create of it, for "spaces where discourses meet agentic actors" (Clarke and Olesen 1999:18)[10] What is distinctive about this approach to textual discourse is that it allows us to examine how the normative construction of motherhood—who gets counted and who does not—is accomplished by women as they engage the norms and messages organized by the discourse.

The move to examine women's relation to objectified discourse is central for feminist studies of medicalization. The heightened sensitivity to women's agency in relation to medical discourse structures much of the recent work because it theorizes medical objectification and women's agency as interdependent. Julia Grant's (1998) analysis of mothers' relation to the discourse of child development found that "most mothers are discriminating consumers who evaluate professional expertise as one body of knowledge to be considered along with existing maternal practices and familial, religious, and community values" (1998:6). Marina Benjamin's (1993) recommendation to examine how women are "enabled to act" within their particular social positions is directly relevant here. Similarly, Smith (1990) argues that even as "objectified" modes of knowing set constraints on women's agency, these are used, deployed, and negotiated by women. Smith conceptualizes discourse as essentially discursive, as a system of meaning and practice generated in and by women in particular social contexts. According to Smith, "Behind the subject in discourse is another subject who is also clearly a member of the discourse, but at another level of its organization . . . [a subject who] speaks from the site of the work behind the appearance" (1990:195).

Medicalized Motherhood focuses on the "subject . . . behind the appearance." My book examines women's narratives as stories of women's agency, in which they embraced, resisted, and transformed the medical appropriation of motherhood. Studying medicalization from the perspective of women's everyday lives exposes the ideology of scientific progress as only a partial perspective on medical discourse. As agents responding to their own needs, constraints, and ambitions, women also give it their own meanings. I take a quintessential sociological approach to the analysis of scientific motherhood; I argue that it is by understanding the uses women made of medical discourse that we can ascertain its significance for motherhood.

DIFFERENCES AMONG WOMEN AND STRUCTURES OF INEQUALITY

Feminist scholarship has taken us a long way toward locating the social production of science, the ways in which science produces motherhood and motherhood produces science. Yet there has been relatively little scholarship on the link between motherhood, science, and ethnoracial inequality, that is, little attention to how women of diverse class and ethnoracial positions related to and were affected by the discourse of scientific motherhood.

Medicalized Motherhood examines how ethnoracial and class inequalities *among women* are both embedded in and constructed through women's relations to medical discourse. Women develop different uses of this discourse depending on the differences in their economic, social, and health-related opportunities as they carry out mother work. Mothering itself is a radically divided social institution, offering some women tremendous social supports in the creation of family life and others tremendous obstacles. As Maxine Baca Zinn states about the disparities among families, "the uneven distribution of social advantages and social costs operates to strengthen some families while simultaneously weakening others" (1994:306).[11] Evelyn Nakano Glenn describes the importance of examining race, gender, and class as inseparable in motherhood precisely because it signifies differences in power: Gender, race, and class "develop in the context of [each] other; they cannot be separated. This is important because when we see reproductive labor only as gendered, we extract gender from its context, which includes other interacting systems of power" (1994:33).

The analytic task which focuses on intersections of identity and power involves "moving beyond gender" in the study of women's relations to medicine (Collins 1999:261). In women's narratives of medicalization we find a struggle between the old and the new, a negotiation over the trajectory of mothering practice and identity. But we also find a contest between social groups over boundaries, status, and acceptability. Women's narratives point to the multiple and contradictory meanings of medical discourse from diverse women's perspectives, showing medical discourse not as a culturally neutral set of technical practices but as a site where social movement and inclusion for some and cultural dislocation and exclusion for others is enacted. We shall see that women's narratives signal much about how structural inequalities impact the creation of gendered identities, relations among women, and meanings of motherhood.

Part I

Encountering Medicine, Constructing Motherhood

Chapter 2

"I Was a Modern Mother"

Americanization and Jewish Women's Medicalization

I don't know about today, but in this area that we're talking about, doctors were idolized and looked upon as gods. You know? If you didn't trust your doctor, you didn't trust anybody.

Elsie Reisner

Elsie Reisner, born in 1894 and the eldest of the Jewish women I interviewed, could hardly contain her enthusiasm for doctors and modern medicine. She embraced the new medical guidelines for child health, the first in her family to do so, with fervor and devotion. In fact, Elsie saw her medicalized mothering practices as signaling her movement beyond the economic and social marginality of her family's immigrant culture. Adopting modern medical techniques proved her Americanization.

This modernizing and medicalized orientation was a style of mothering that Elsie cultivated; it occupied a great portion of her mothering practice. As attractive as Elsie found it, it was not without its dilemmas. Elsie describes a conflict between her modern orientation and the traditional one preferred by her immigrant mother-in-law, a conflict that emerged as a contest over who and which practices defined the household:

> The baby had jaundice. So the doctor said to me "Fill him with water." So I put water in a bottle and I boiled water and cooled

[it] and I gave it to him. My mother-in-law, behind my back, would take [the bottle] with her dirty hands and put sugar in the thing and get it all over the nipple and stick it in his mouth. She didn't want him to drink water that wasn't sweetened.

It was not only to the sweetened water (a common traditional practice) that Elsie objected, but also to her mother-in-law's disregard for the new standards of cleanliness that she had learned in school:

Where I would wash my hands with the blink of an eye, [my mother-in-law] would put her hands into something else and the same hands into this and that and it annoyed me. . . . When I went to school, now we had cooking lessons and they emphasized cleanliness and the washing of the hands and cleansing of clean towels and clean this and clean that. And I wanted it, so I absorbed it. I liked what the doctor was doing. I can change very fast even today. And that's how I went along with it.

Elsie constructed her mothering as a rejection of the old practices (e.g. dirty hands and sweetened water) and an acceptance of the new (e.g. boiling water, cleanliness, and the doctor). She tied her practice to the education for motherhood she received in school and in her consultations with the doctor. And she saw herself as "absorbing" new ideas and as "changing" with the times, mirroring the early-twentieth-century belief that women were emissaries of scientific progress and that Jewish women's immigrant practices were both backward and dangerous to children (Cowan and Cowan 1989; Ewen 1985; Isaacs 1941; Kraut 1994; Rose 1994). Linking herself to the momentum of social change and progress, Elsie positioned herself as a modern and successful mother.

Yet Elsie also used medical discourse to establish her everyday control in the household. Turning to the doctor—and borrowing his authority—gave her some leverage to manage the conflict with her mother-in-law:

My mother-in-law would come in and take it all into her own hands and that was it. So I had to put a stop to it. And the next time the baby cried, that's it. I went to the doctor. I wanted to know what to do without dirty hands in front of my face handling everything that I was so careful with. . . . I didn't insult her, I didn't jump at her. This is all I said to her. "Just let me raise mine." And then I got myself out of there and I started to turn to the doctor. So what could she say? [Doctors] were looked up to, they were respected. You wouldn't think of doubting a word if it came out of a doctor's mouth.

Elsie's narrative points to the complex meanings of medicalized mothering for the Jewish women in this study. Far from occupying a simple and value-neutral set of recommendations for health, medicine signaled much about Elsie's social position and domestic control in the new landscape of Americanization. In her everyday life, medical discourse represented more than scientific fact; it held out the promise of a new identity and household culture, and equipped her, in the context of generational and cultural tensions and her own social ambitions, with the necessary household authority to create her mothering and family in ways that followed the new social expectations. She developed a medicalized culture of mothering as she negotiated the social relations of her Americanization.

Migrancy, identity, and cultural transformation are recurrent themes in Jewish women's narratives of medicalization. Medicalization figured in women's lives as an expression of their negotiations of these complex personal experiences of change and motherhood and came to represent both an opportunity and a necessity for their social acceptance. The African-American respondents also represent their mothering as organized along the tensions and promises of migration and identity, although it is largely the upwardly mobile women for whom medical discourse represented a symbol of social advance. The diasporic quality common to the Jewish and African-American women's mothering narratives, however striking, fits with their respective ethnoracial histories of persecution and marginality (Cowan and Cowan 1989; Hine 1996; Hyman 1994; Lewis 1996). These struggles and self-definitions were relevant to women's creations of mothering cultures: it was through their condition of migrancy that women enacted their relations to dominant social and cultural codes. And it was also from this position that women gave medical discourse, the premiere symbol of social membership and acknowledgment, its social meaning.

All eighteen Jewish women that I interviewed were the daughters of immigrants from eastern Europe, so-called Russians, with the exception of one whose mother was born in Philadelphia. Six of the women's parents migrated as married couples, and in four cases the fathers came first, sending for their wives and children once they had a job and living quarters. Three of the women I interviewed (Estelle Sein, Essa Goldschmidt, and Vivian Harris) were immigrants themselves, having come to the United States with their parents from Russia when they were small children.

Once they came of age in America, the fathers of my respondents established their own small businesses (as carpenters, grocers, paper hangers, sign painters, tailors) or worked in the garment industry. Their mothers were typically full-time housewives, although some worked in the family businesses. By and large, immigrant women had limited contact with the dominant, non-Jewish world, knew less English than their husbands and children, and developed fewer connections to Americanization than others in their households. Because of their relative social isolation, most immigrant women of this generation had few opportunities to be "real Americans" (Weinberg 1988:106).[1] We shall see that this created particular tensions for their daughters, the second-generation immigrants that I interviewed, whose daily lives were directed explicitly toward assimilation (Cowan and Cowan 1989).[2] Before we examine how these women used their motherhood practices to create their new status as Americans, however, we need to understand the social context of their own childhoods, where they learned the value of Americanization and medicine and the backwardness of immigrant culture.

Looking Back: Russian Persecution, Social Marginality, and Health Practices

And we came to America. Oh, when we came to
America we literally, my brother and I, fell down and
kissed the ground. Oh, we were, oh God, we were in
heaven. This is America! And we landed on Ellis Island
in New York. And when the boat took us to New York
and we got off there and we saw all the people and it was
so lively and bright. And we just couldn't believe it, that
there was such a thing in the world. And we just loved it,
America. America was just wonderful. We were free.

We didn't have to live in one little place. You know, all
the Jews lived in a little cove. And uh, [in America] we
were like everybody else. We were people, real people.

Estelle Sein

For Estelle, who came to the United States with her mother when she
was a young girl, the journey to America represented emergence from
persecution; she speaks of movement, of brightness, of liveliness, and
especially, of becoming "real people" in America. This belief stemmed
from the abysmal conditions she and her family had fled in Russia. By
the turn of the twentieth century the Russian economy was deeply in
debt and had slowed considerably in comparison to Western European
industry. The Pale settlements (the fifteen western districts of Russia
and the ten districts of Russian Poland), to which most of Russia's five
million Jews were confined, fared even worse than Russia in general,
particularly between 1881 and the 1917 revolution when most of the
migration took place. The anti-Semitism toward Jews in Russia was but-
tressed by constricted residential and occupational rights, the official
sanctioning of pogroms, and the liberalizing of emigration policies for
Jews. Much of the Jewish population migrated in these years, either from
rural to urban ghettos in Pale settlements or out of Russia altogether
(Friedman-Kasaba 1996).

The lack of access to scientific advances was one feature of their
persecution, and many women understood that migration to America
meant the possibility of improved health (Kraut 1994). Sarah Rosenfeld,
for example, understands her parents' migration from Russia as a health
issue, "for the sake of the baby":

> I think my mother lost two children in Russia. So when my
> brother was born, they packed up and came to America. He was
> about six weeks old when they arrived. I understand [my father]
> went berserk when [the children died]. And I guess . . . they left
> Russia to come here for the sake of the baby, I imagine.

It was common in the interviews for the mothers to talk of the lack of
medical care for their parents' families in Russia. They spoke a great
deal of the pogroms, of the forced confinement of Jews in the Pale settlements, and of the need for Jews to escape from certain death and in-
jury in Russia. And they associated persecution with poor health.
Indeed, in Russia, typhus, smallpox, and cholera hit Jews particularly

hard (Kraut 1994). Physicians were unavailable. Food was scarce. Illnesses persisted. America, in the minds of immigrants, offered the possibility of health and access to medical care.

In the following excerpt, Judith Kleinman, raised by her immigrant grandparents in the United States, explains the implications for parenting that Russian persecution created:

> I don't know how [my grandmother] raised her children. In the
> old country, as far as I can remember from seeing movies of
> these small villages, the kids [were] running around barefooted
> on a muddy floor, no floors in the houses. They lived in huts.
> They were persecuted. All of a sudden the Cossacks would
> come and raid the place. They hated Jews. . . . A lot of people
> ran away from Russia because of that. They call it the pogroms.
> So how could they worry about how they're raising children?

Judith points to the use of Russian home remedies as a survival strategy in the face of persecution:

> I don't think that people in the circumstances that our parents
> or grandparents were in thought too much about [going to
> doctors]. They only believed in home remedies because they
> didn't have doctors over where they came from. It was all home
> remedies, grandmother remedies. Some of them worked
> probably but . . . they didn't have doctors over there. They were
> persecuted. They were not allowed to go to school.

In describing her use of modern remedies for raising her own family, Judith sees herself as "smarter" and more in "control" in comparison with her elders' experiences of child care:

> [My grandparents] thought the [old] remedies worked because
> they brought it over from the old country. They were unedu-
> cated. They didn't read. I had an education. I was able to see
> the right of things and the wrong part of things and I couldn't
> see anything that would be beneficial to any of my kids. Wrap
> them with a piece of potato around their head. That's ridicu-
> lous. I had no control over how I was treated [as a child]. But I
> sure did have control over the way I treated my children. I
> think my generation became smarter than my mother's genera-
> tion. Being more knowledgeable about taking care of children,
> raising them. I wasn't raised up I was dragged up.

Judith draws on contemporary cultural images of America as the place of refuge for persecuted Jews of Russia. She expands this association by adding access to scientific advance as one benefit of living in this new world of economic, social, and religious safety. In this narrative, the life without persecution that America offered is tantamount to a life that focuses on children's good health, and that allows her more control as a mother.

Yet many immigrants did not immediately embrace the new medical ways. In the following narrative, Elsie associates her immigrant mother's social marginality with her distance from medical discourse, even in her new home in Philadelphia:

> My mother had stepped on a rusty nail and I can still see that happening. I must have been about three years old. And my uncle brought in Dr. Ludwig Berg to treat my mother at home. And he knew looking at this patient of his that she would not go to the hospital and he operated [on] her on the kitchen table. You know?

I asked Elsie whether her mother did not believe in hospitals. She responded:

> You are talking about people that came out of a country where they existed, they didn't live. They just existed. They were mistreated. They were beaten. They were killed. They were not respected. Or haven't you heard?

Elsie considered it enough of an explanation of her mother's hesitation about hospitals to say to me—in increasingly agitated terms—that hospitals were unthinkable, unfamiliar places for these people who "didn't live," who "just existed." Elsie represents her mother as perceiving medicine only from its periphery, precisely because her status as an immigrant confined her to a permanent condition of social marginality even in the United States. Many immigrant Jews, in fact, continued to suffer the negative health effects produced by crowded tenement life, although they also had lower morbidity and infant mortality rates than other native and ethnoracial minority groups (Condran and Preston 1994; Kraut 1994). Elsie's own "adaptability" and invention of new, healthy mothering practices depended on her belief that she had overcome the socially marginal position rendered by immigration.

In these narratives of the hardship of Russian and immigrant life for their parents, we find women expressing collective stories about their past and future. As the daughters of immigrants, they shared a social and historical space and established a common perception of the past and of what was possible and desirable in the new country. The stories they tell of geographic and social movement are as much reflections of their personal ideals of maternal responsibility as they are reports of objective conditions in Russia or in America (Bottomley 1992).

The narrations about Russian persecution and hardship in immigrant America act as a frame against which the Jewish women I interviewed defined their mothering. Their mothering narratives focus on their negotiations of their liminal social status, situated between the immigrant generation and the new, Americanizing one. They employed medical discourse as one of several dominant codes that represented and enacted their work of Americanizing. And for these women who embraced and felt they had to carry out modern principles of mothering, medical discourse represented both a unique opportunity and a special obligation; it was their responsibility to use their new economic and social advantage to create American households. Medicalization equipped women to enact their Americanization; it also compelled them to do so.

Women learned growing up that Americanization and modernization were necessary for social acceptability, and that they were women's work. As we saw in chapter 1, the response to the influx of immigrants in the late nineteenth and early twentieth centuries produced an Americanization discourse which, in its dominant form, stressed the link between health, mothers' household practices, and ethnoracial status. It was not only secular or Christian settlement institutions that established this approach toward Americanization. Philadelphia had its own Jewish settlement projects; a major one was The Neighborhood Center, which for much of its history directed its courses and programs toward teaching Jewish mothers new, scientific approaches to cooking, shopping, feeding, and child care (Rose 1994). Manuals written by Jewish authors for Jewish mothers also warned women of their obligation to partake in American advances, but to do so in the context of Jewish institutions (Isaacs 1941; Joselit 1994).

Anti-Semitism and anti-immigration sentiment in the first decades of the twentieth century often took the form of labeling Jews as inferior biologically, degenerate, and a public health menace (Kraut 1994). In his analysis of the link between "germs, genes, and the 'immigrant menace'" in public health screening, Alan M. Kraut documents how nativist prejudice was "medicalized." Health was used to mark the insider from the outsider; "unhealthy" was the metaphor used to define the excludable.

The value placed on new health practices and cultural assimilation thus contained powerful messages about Jewish acceptability. Philadelphia's Jewish institutions of the 1920s and 1930s mirrored these concerns. As we might expect, moreover, Philadelphia's Jewish community and institutional life were divided (Rose 1994).[3] Russian immigrants encountered tense relationships with established middle-class Jews, as historian Elizabeth Rose explains: "[W]hen East European immigrants encountered German Jews, each group brought with them a different understanding of what it meant to be Jewish in America" (1994:6). Many German Jews in the United States had achieved economic and social security by the late nineteenth century and perceived the large influx of Jewish immigrants from Eastern Europe as a threat to their inclusion in the social mainstream. A leading Philadelphia Rabbi explained to his fellow German Jews that the Russian Europeans held "Habits repulsive to propriety [and] . . . sentiments foreign to civilization. . . . [W]ink at it, let it go unchecked, and you will imperil the good reputation of Philadelphia Hebrews most seriously" (quoted in Rose 1994:7). In response, German Jews in Philadelphia established philanthropic organizations that were geared toward helping immigrants and their children assimilate to life in America (Baltzell et al. 1983; Rose 1994; Rosen 1983). German-Jewish women were especially active in the movement to establish settlement projects to Americanize Jewish immigrant families newly arrived from Eastern Europe. A founder of one such Philadelphia organization recommended directing the focus on children: "It was felt that to make of the children good American citizens to imbue them with the best American ideals, would be work that would ultimately give the best results" (quoted in Rose 1994:7).

The public health movement, settlement projects, Jewish institutional activity, and public school lessons came together to create a cultural climate where the assimilation of immigrants into American life held supreme value. The Jewish respondents in this study grew up in this context and were exposed, as children and young adults, to the message of Americanization and modernization. Their narratives tell the story of balancing between two worlds: the world of their mothers and other elders, who typically continued to validate traditional practice in regard to baby care, and the world of modernity, where medical discourse held primary authority. Using medical discourse to guide their own mothering constituted an engagement with the modern style of mothering these women wanted to adopt, but it demanded a simultaneous weakening of their allegiance to the ways of their parents, especially their mothers.

Becoming Modern Mothers: Linking Position and Practice

Just because your mother and your grandmother did it I didn't think that was the best thing. I was a modern mother and the modern way was to go to a specialist.

Mimi Rubin

Despite the financial turmoil and setbacks created by the Great Depression and the ups and downs of their own economic situations, the Jewish women almost uniformly defined themselves as more financially and socially secure than their parents had been, a status improvement they saw as essential to their modernization. Economic security alone, however, did not signal new identities or status for Jewish mothers; rather, much of the work of transforming their new economic position into new social standing required mothers' conscious attention to status work, to what Randall Collins (1992) calls the production of status cultures.

The practices involved in creating class position entailed, of course, access to wages, which for most Jewish women were supplied by their husbands. Many were eventually able, with their husbands, to purchase their own homes and to move out of Jewish immigrant neighborhoods to suburban or other metropolitan areas that they saw as middle class and upwardly mobile. And most women did not have to seek paid employment when their children were young, as their husbands' salaries were often sufficient to support their new lifestyles. Yet economic production, which fell primarily to men in these households, was only one element in the production of middle-class status. Cultural status production, the province of housewives and mothers, also was central to making these households middle class.

I take a view of social-class relations that stresses their dynamic character. Rather than reflect a household's economic position, social-class relations involve daily negotiations and practice. According to Marjorie DeVault, class relations "organize the activities of individuals and families both in very direct ways—such as through the wages flowing into households or the demands of particular occupations—[and] in less direct ways, through [social] locations in particular neighborhoods, schools, and other social groups (1991:168). Women are central to this stratification system because of their domestic position, which involves them in forging connections with institutions of social mobility (such as neighborhoods, schools, and medicine). Class relations pattern and are patterned by women's household work; through mothers' household practices, women are implicated in the production of class as well as gender (Collins 1992; Smith 1984).

Much the same can be said for achieving an American identity. Incorporation into American ways is not a static process. Nor is it ungendered. Rather, Jewish women's narratives depict the process of social inclusion as ongoing, as dependent on their own work of making the transformation from old to new. This work of identity creation and status negotiation helped to forge Jewish women's ties to medical discourse.

Mothers' narratives show mothers performing the socially necessary but largely invisible work of becoming socially mainstream. The trust in scientific progress, already a "central article of the dominant American faith" (LaFollette 1990:9), involved for these women a set of work requirements for personal and household transformation. Barbara Schwartz, whose immigrant childhood household was more modern than others, gives us an insider's look at this work of transformation:

> [The American way] was to develop, to progress, to reach out.
> We heard concerts, my parents went. We went to the museums,
> the library at Nineteenth Street and the Parkway. We did all
> that. I mean we reached out. . . . My older sister [an immigrant]

would read to my mother since my mother couldn't read. I
recall . . . that my sister had a Shakespearean book with
passages underlined. That is no marvel, but that she did it
without the American education is remarkable. Absolutely
remarkable. The words that he put down, that Shakespeare put
down in his plays made such a vast impression on her. That it
makes an impression on me should be no miracle. To her, who
was an immigrant, with all of that before her, that took a lot of
doing, a lot of wanting to know. There was a culture in the
household.

While it might seem unusual to invoke Shakespeare as a cultural symbol of Americanization, Barbara did so by making the link between education, advance, and the shedding of immigrant ignorance. Her mother
too was invested in Americanization and used a whole series of personal and social improvements—using nail polish, traveling, reading—
to cultivate it:

My mother was trying to become Americanized . . . with
[sending us to] school, with nail polish, with traveling on her
own without being able to read. [She] went to Chicago to a spa
there. That's developing. To wanting to look well, to dress,
that's important, very important.

But it was in her own mother work that Barbara felt she was able
to move beyond this provisional space of her parents' household. She
comments about her reluctance to seek her parents' advice about child
care:

Uh, well no. And I'll tell you why. . . . The attitude, at least for
me, was they're European. They don't know the American way.
[My parents] were European, you know, with no experience.
But that of course is incorrect. They really had practical
experience. But I was too uptight or too young to recognize
that. Or too willing to accept the American way. Could be.

Barbara explains "the American way":

Oh well, part of our way of life. I don't know. I can't put that
into words but you knew that you didn't want the European
way, you knew that, even though they could be right. I never
even thought of them being right.

Barbara states that it was not scientific truth as much as status and a "way of life" that was at stake in medicalization. Even though she saw her childhood household as more socially advanced (read: Americanized) than others, she still found it necessary to resist her parents' practices. These practices, whether right or wrong, symbolized another culture, another time, and another place—making them unsuitable for her situation of motherhood. Here we see how deeply women's understandings of their own mothering practices were tied to their investment in securing their social standing. What mattered less to them, and what they had no power to evaluate, was the technical right and wrong of the practices; what they could evaluate about traditional remedies was the symbolic meaning of their use. And it was on this ground that these modernizing mothers rejected the traditional.

We find this pattern also in Rose Kleiner's description of her refusal to follow her immigrant mother-in-law's customs:

> I never took my mother-in-law's remedies. She came from the other side. I mean, after all, we're American. We're not from the little shtetla. I [had] the biggest man [doctor] in the city when Phyllis was born. So this is who I felt had more knowledge than old-fashioned remedies. I didn't use old-fashioned remedies. It wasn't my way of living. I wanted to know what we do today. Not what we did thirty, forty years ago. What good was thirty, forty years ago? You have to know today.

Both Rose and Barbara construct narratives of status negotiation where their participation in scientific progress provided the basis for their redefined social position. They raise a division between what was "old-fashioned" and "what we do today," identifying a trajectory of "knowledge" that advances and that should be applied to everyday living. What is significant is that their Americanization depended first on their sense of their own inclusion in this social movement of progress. Rather than watch from the sidelines, these women considered modernization as applicable to them.

Sarah Rosenfeld, the daughter of immigrants and the mother of three, vividly portrays the tension that this created with her mother:

> I had moved to the second-floor bedroom apartment in my parents' house and the baby'd be crying. Well, [the baby] was

due to get her next feeding at two o'clock, and if it was five of two, she cried. I was a perfect mother, no reason why. The hospital sent you home with a list and they told you exactly what to do. . . . [My mother] used to come up and knock on the apartment door. I locked her out. And she called me a murderer. I remember her saying it in Jewish, "It doesn't cost you anything, I'll pay you, give her some milk." This was the way it had to be. If [the doctor] said every four hours, every four hours. It was the right thing to do. I had a little bolt on my door and she couldn't come in.

Creating the gap between the feeding practices of her mother and her own, more medically oriented, techniques took on this weight precisely because Sarah, like other mothers, saw her identity and social position at stake. Through this work of using technical and scientific resources, she could create her household as American, as middle class, and as a participant in the momentum of social progress.

Yet access to medical advances in America was not only celebrated. It also signaled a new obligation. Given its normative value, the medicalized culture these mothers developed raised a series of routine demands and stances toward motherhood that they felt obliged to meet. Not surprisingly, themes of obedience figure large in these women's narratives of medicalized motherhood. Lori Ragowitz, the daughter of immigrants and mother of three, explains the protocol demanded by this medical regimen:

We would go to Dr. Stewart once a month, you know, to keep track of things. Weight and change of formula, change of this, when to put him on solids and things like that. You know, the normal stuff. . . . There was no one else to ask. That was the thing to do at that particular time because it was getting to be the norm. To take your kid to a doctor right from the beginning, to see that everything was all right, to do what has to be done.[4]

Lori treats feeding along with weight and general checkups as one of many medicalized activities that brought her mothering routine under the guidance of outside experts. What she, along with Barbara, Rose, and Sarah, reveals is that her creation of acceptable mothering was daily work that required submission to expert knowledge.

These women constructed their relation to doctors as one way to measure their acceptability as mothers. Diane Weinberg, the daughter of immigrants and mother of one, identifies the role the physician's house call played in establishing her as a good mother:

> And [the doctor] would walk up the steps [to the apartment]. He didn't do that to everybody. And he knew that I'm the kind of mother that will be there. Sometimes he would get to people's apartments and he'd never go back again to their home. They wouldn't be there. There was a maid to show him the child's room. . . . He liked me because he knew I was interested. Not only interested, but worried.

Diane shows the interrelation between her desire for acceptability, the doctor's demands, and normative standards for motherhood. She narrates a story of maternal success in the terms of American middle-class domesticity; she was not only available to her children and the doctor but different from those mothers who were not. In this, she also narrates a story of maternal obligation, where the very basis for social acceptance depended on compliance with these daily expectations.

Opportunity and Obligation: Two Narratives

[The doctors] had to tell you what to feed her. I mean, every month they gave her something else, I mean. First, it was a bottle, then it was cereal, then it was fruits and vegetables and then it was meats, and then they had to get their shots, a vaccination, and then they had to get the whooping cough shots and then the diphtheria shots and the tetanus and all that. And you had to go. You went once a month and they weighed them and they checked them and they told you what foods you could give them.

Selma Cohen

Born in Philadelphia in 1918 to Jewish parents who emigrated from Russia as children, Selma Cohen positioned her reliance on medicine as an obligation—"you had to go." For Selma this orientation signaled her advance away from a difficult childhood. Her parents separated when she was fifteen, at which point her mother opened a small store to support herself and the children. At twenty years old, Selma married a Jewish man in the scrap metal business. She had two children, a daughter born in 1940 and a son five years later.

Like the other Jewish women, Selma represents her mothering practice as deeply indebted to experts, books, and science:

> [The books] made you feel safer that you had something to know, you know. You were doing the right thing, you know. You were going by somebody who knew better than you. I followed everything to the letter.

Doing so, according to Selma, made her like "everybody" else:

> Everybody did the same thing [went to physicians]. There was some people who maybe wouldn't. They'd say well their mother would tell them what to do, and this and that, but I was very ethical and I thought that's what you're supposed to do and that's what I was doing.

Selma, in fact, was not as much interested in being like "everybody" else as much as being like other "ethical" (read: modern, assimilated) mothers with whom she wished to identify. Yet her narrative also reveals how medicine's recommendations became obligatory, even coercive. She described in vivid detail the struggles she encountered in feeding her children:

> Of course [my daughter] was a horrible eater, so even though [the doctor] told me what to give, she didn't eat anyway. Oh, it was horrible, I mean, just feeding her was the most atrocious thing you ever wanted to do. That's why I didn't have another child 'til five years later, because she was such a horrible eater. I thought I didn't want a second one. But when I had my son, I thought she was bad—he was ten times worse.

Her narrative of feeding her children was dominated by her feelings of frustration, fear, and self-sacrifice:

> And he [my son] was the world's worst. He didn't eat anything. And all he did want was his bottle. Know how I used to feed my son? You'll have to laugh. He would lay down, he'd be laying down on the table and he'd open his mouth for the bottle, but

he didn't want food. So I couldn't hold him because I had to use two hands to do the manipulation. I put him on the table, lay him down, had the spoon in one hand, bottle in the other, he'd open his mouth for the bottle and when he opened up for the bottle, I'd put the spoon in there and that's how he ate his food.

Selma reveals a tension between her sense of responsibility about how much food she was told her child was supposed to eat and the real-life frustrations she encountered when feeding him. Her characterization of these difficulties and her elaborate description of the effort she expended to overcome them make explicit what medical discourse hides—both the work involved in fitting one's mothering practices to medical standards and the emotional consequences of failing to meet them. Indeed, Selma was not comforted by her physician's assurances that her son was not in danger because she saw that other women were able to carry out his expectations; watching other mothers feed their children with ease, Selma was burdened with feelings of inadequacy:

I went down to ninety-two pounds. . . . I used to see other people feeding their children and the children would eat everything in sight and mine just didn't well, you know you don't sleep and you don't eat right. I was never very much of an eater, but you're taking care of a baby who doesn't eat and you're worried about him 'cause he doesn't eat and he doesn't sleep. So you, you know, you don't really take care of yourself very much.

Through her "manipulations" Selma attempted to bridge the gap between the normative expectations of compliance and the realities of her daily life. It is certainly ironic that a discourse Selma describes as "making you feel safer" functioned as a sign of her frustrations and failure.

Selma's fears, rooted in her pervasive and virtually debilitating sense of obligation, were precisely what the doctor ordered. In medical discourse, the household and mothers were a site of danger for children. While positioned as the primary site where children could (and should) be protected from the outside world and its various contaminants (including mothers' nonmedical knowledge), the household was also constructed as potentially destructive to child health. Proper medical supervision, doctors warned, was a mother's only hope to establish her children's health. By viewing herself as responsible for incorporating these new standards into her everyday practice, Selma evaluated and often criticized her own activities.

Edna Levin's narrative illustrates also the tension between obligation and opportunity. She focused on how her household became a site for the physician's evaluation of motherhood. The daughter of immigrants and mother of two, Edna delighted in the fact that her child's physician made house calls. She paid five dollars a visit, money well spent for her children's safety: "Well, at that time [the children] were more susceptible at catching what some other child may have. . . . So it was better when they came to the house." Her fears of contagion and danger beyond the household provided a context against which the house call emerged as desirable. Subjecting her routines to direct scrutiny by the physician was not a burden that she merely tolerated, but rather a benefit she demanded.

At the same time, the house call permitted the physician's scrutiny of Edna's household. She describes an encounter she had with her doctor, one which reveals the connection between medicine's meaning for her social status and for her sense of obligation:

> You know you read baby magazines. How to take care of your baby and all. And I had them on my chair in my bedroom. [Dr. Weidman] walked in, he said, I'll never forget, "If you want me to be your doctor, you'll get rid of all those magazines."

Edna explains her initial attraction to these magazines:

> When you're a new mother, you think you're gonna learn about breast-feeding and things of that sort. . . . There were different kinds of bottles then, at the time, different foods, the baby foods. And they all would advertise it. . . . [But he said] "I don't want you to use those anymore." . . . I kept telling people about it. I was impressed that he even noticed that I had magazines there.

Edna explains why the doctor was so insistent:

> Because he had his own way to do things. And when he spoke to you, it was him, not reading it in a magazine. And I guess

sometimes you'll read something and then they don't agree with what he said. So he said, "You'll just get rid of them." I said [to myself], "I'll see if I like him or not. Then I'll see what will happen." And, uh, it's a shame he's not around anymore. He wasn't one of these that came in all dressed up, you know, and all this. And he wasn't a real handsome man. But when he spoke to you, you listened to him. He was *hamish* [modest, ordinary]. . . . He came in and my mother used to make sour pickles. He'd like a sour pickle with his sandwich and he'd sit down and he'd talk to you. And any questions you had, he would answer you.

Edna normalizes the physician's regulation and investigation as part of the round of events that medical attention demanded:

I didn't resent it. . . . You know, as far as that. It's just that [the magazines] were out on a chair in the bedroom. And we walked in the bedroom. And he saw them there. No, I wasn't insulted or resented it or anything. I just thought it was funny that he noticed them and [he] said, "If you want me to be your doctor you'll get rid of them." So I said, "Okay." Because I heard that he was a good pediatrician, and I was glad that I was able to get him because he was in a great deal of demand. . . . I didn't bother with them anymore. And then when I would see anybody else with them, I would tell 'em the same thing. "If you want Dr. Weidman, you'd better not have those magazines here." My sister never read them. She wanted him to come to her house. So she would never have the magazines.

Edna's investment in Dr. Weidman's involvement in her household smoothed over whatever insult could have been perceived in his intrusion into her privacy. Indeed, his surveillance impressed her: "I was impressed that he even noticed." Her narrative of the desirability and requirements of the house call, like the narratives of other women we met in this chapter, was one of fostering a household in the physician's image of acceptability. Edna asserts her agency in positioning herself as capable of evaluating his performance. Yet this was a performance that secured more than health; it was physicians who women used to mediate their new social position, helping them secure their positions as good, American mothers.

The Jewish women I interviewed raised their children in a context where medical discourse acquired institutional and cultural authority over the health practices of immigrant households and communities. It was a discourse in which Jewish claims to assimilation rested. It was in the private domain of the household that the women's health work was to be performed, in essence making the household and mother work not only the objects of medical intervention for child health but also the measures of Jewish acceptability. For women invested in securing their place in the dominant society, everyday health practices, from hygiene habits to feeding techniques, took on enormous social significance.

Constructing acceptable households required women to take on child care as a private, family responsibility, where they distanced themselves from the advice and caretaking help of other women (except when this advice and help encouraged medicalization). They also viewed the household as a haven from disease and took great pains to establish the purity of their own domestic units, borrowing the cultural authority of medicine in doing so. Here too, we find a level of vigilance that gained its power from the status negotiations it implied. Returning to Elsie's narrative, which opened this chapter, we see cleanliness and dirt constituting the boundaries marking insider from outsider (Douglas 1966).

Medical discourse is a cultural form among others, not a privileged category of knowledge that stands apart from cultural codes or practice. Jewish women encountered medical discourse and constructed medicalization not only as a system of technical knowledge but also as a social practice through which they measured and produced their status position. Medicine's claim to scientific expertise was interpreted through the lens of their collective histories and personal trajectories of social exclusion and inclusion.

Medicalized motherhood is, as other scholars have noted, a primary way to socialize women into the dominant standards of the time. Yet by looking at how women create medicalization, by treating medicalization as a process, not as a discrete entity, we find that it is not as passive victims but as agents that women encounter and give meaning to this discourse. Medicalization offered women the appearance and perception of social belonging and acceptability, while fastening their motherhood to dominant codes.

Chapter 3	"My Mother Was with Me All the Time"

The Southern Context of African-American Women's Medicalization

My aunt was a midwife. She delivered most of my kids. She would [tie] a sheet to the bedpost. And she give you the end of it. And when you have a pain, you pull on that sheet. Every time you have a pain you just pull on that sheet and bear down [and when] that pain was over you just let go 'til you felt another pain coming. . . . And [the family] be sittin' in the living room. And . . . nobody knows I was having a baby until they hear the baby cry.

Reather Herbert

The majority of African-American women in my study came to Philadelphia in the Great Migration, the massive shift in the U.S. African-American population in the first four decades of this century from South to North. Philadelphia was one of many cities that enjoyed a massive influx of migrants: the total African-American population of Philadelphia went from 134,229 in 1916 to 219,599 in 1929, an increase of 64 percent, two-thirds of whom came from the South. And between 1910 and 1940 Philadelphia's African-American population almost tripled (McBride 1989). The principal reasons for the migration changed in the course of this period, but most migrants had in common an experience of economic deprivation, political disfranchisement, racial hatred, and violence in the South and a desire for better jobs (Marks 1989).[1] Jim Crow laws kept the social and economic inequalities securely in place in the South; the promise of an open economy in the North exerted a strong attraction for African-American men and women who hoped to escape them.

Coming North was not, however, an easy experience, as a great deal of scholarship documents (Hine 1996).[2] According to Gates, those who came North in the Great Migration hoping to forge new economic and social lives were inducted "into the technological America of the twentieth century as if . . . transported in a time machine" (1993:18). Reather Herbert's experience confirms Gates's contention; she first encountered modern methods of childbirth when she came to Philadelphia, arriving much later than the typical migrant, in 1959. In her home of Greenville, North Carolina, she consulted her aunt, a midwife, for the delivery of her first child in 1935 and for the twelve children thereafter. She raised these children with the help of her mother, stepfather, and siblings whose household she shared. When she moved to Philadelphia at the age of forty-one, she found herself facing entirely new circumstances of mothering.

Like many migrant women, Reather moved to Philadelphia alone; Reather, in fact, left her children with her family in North Carolina. After living with her sister in a small apartment for one year, Reather became involved with a man, and together they sent for the children. She had three more children once in Philadelphia. Below she describes the birthing experience she underwent in Philadelphia, one that speaks to a kind of social dislocation as much as physical violation:

> [In the hospital] every ten minutes, here come the doctor with
> them gloves on, sticking his finger and arms up ya, and you're
> [more] sore when they get through with you [than] when you
> just have a baby by yourself. . . . Time you didn't have a pain,
> here come the doctor and here, "Let me see, honey." Yeah. And
> then boy that pain gonna hear the other pain comin'. And
> then sometime, you know pain, when you really 'bout labor,
> you can doze off to sleep. And sometime you doze off here, the
> doctor come over here and see you and, ah, I'd rather have a
> midwife anytime.

Reather expresses a sense of indignity in describing this scene, where the doctor rather than trusted family provided the context of her delivery. She tells a story of her rhythm interrupted, broken, and shaped to the physician's whims. She employs a language not of trust, safety, and control, which predominate in her depiction of childbirth in the South, but of violation and invasion. Reather's experience was hardly singular. Reports of uncertainty, fear, and fragile ties to northern medical institutions were common in my interviews with migrant African-American working-class women. Unlike the upwardly mobile Jewish women for whom medical discourse emerged as a means of status advancement and as a symbol of new social inclusion, most of the African-American women I interviewed stressed themes of isolation and alienation as they narrated their experience with medical discourse.

Of the twenty African-American women I interviewed, sixteen were born in the South, most in the Carolinas (see appendix). These women moved to Philadelphia at various stages in their lives: Marion Marks and Gloria Jones arrived in Philadelphia as infants, in 1909 and 1913, respectively; Clara Franks, Lucy Alston, Tessie Woodall, and Phyllis Taylor moved when they were in their teens and twenties, in the middle 1930s; and the remaining ten women moved as young mothers in the 1940s, although Ruth Cooper went in 1956 and Reather Herbert in 1959. It is this latter group of ten that is the focus of this chapter.

The ten migrant mothers I interviewed encountered a system of health care in Philadelphia that was defined and institutionalized in radically new terms: hospitalization with white doctors and nurses replaced home births with African-American midwives (Fraser 1998; Lee 1996; Snow 1993), ingredients for traditional remedies were less available (Snow 1993), and massive urban public health outreach efforts conveyed the superiority of dominant medical practices over traditional healing techniques (Carson 1994; McBride 1989; Smith 1995). Access to medicine and the elimination of racism in medicine were promulgated by African-American leadership, who considered the improvement of health as fundamental to civil rights as were expanded economic and social opportunities (Carson 1994; McBride 1989; Smith 1995). Yet for many women who confronted this new system of treatment with few resources and with a longing for traditional relations of healing, alienation and fear predominated.

The strains that geographical and social change placed on their mothering was never far from the surface in the narratives of the women featured in this chapter. In contrast to the Jewish women we met in chapter 2, these were first-generation migrants, most of whom lacked the social and economic resources to orient their households to modern standards of motherhood. They spoke of a style of motherhood that was embedded in tradition, not in formal texts, and they assigned medical personnel and institutions marginal significance in their daily practices of caretaking. These women maintained a culture of motherhood that was tied closely to the past, rather than predicated on its rejection; that they raised their children in the North did not lessen the place held in their narratives by the experiences, knowledge, and relations of the South, which were, for them, the lifelong framework for mothering.

The women gave various reasons for moving to Philadelphia, but most of them hoped for better jobs and lives for themselves, their husbands, or other family members. Of the ten women, three (Mildred James, Cheryl O'Neil, and Jamie Rivers) came to Philadelphia with their husbands. Two of these husbands were employed at major Philadelphia industries as drivers. The third did farm work. The remaining seven women moved as single mothers. All of the ten women were employed; two were employed in the garment trades and the remaining eight did domestic, kitchen, or laundry work. All took advantage of kin or old-neighborhood ties when they relocated to the North. And all found life in Philadelphia much harder than they had expected.

The economic situation in Philadelphia for African-American migrants certainly did not meet expectations. Each wave of migrants faced structural racial discrimination and experienced eventual job displacement (Marks 1989). During World War I, migrants, promised positions in war industries, found themselves in competition with white ethnoracial immigrants whom employers generally favored. During the Depression the worsened agricultural situation in the South (the replacement of sharecropping by a wage labor system) compelled many more African Americans to migrate North, but they could find only marginal opportunities for stable employment in Philadelphia. In fact, African Americans in Philadelphia felt economic deprivation years before the stock market crash of 1929, and through the 1930s African Americans in Philadelphia had markedly higher rates of unemployment than native and foreign-born whites (McBride 1989). Langston Hughes's

1932 migration poem "Po' Boy Blues" is an apt representation of how many experienced this encounter with the North:

> When I was home de
>   Sunshine seemed like gold.
> When I was home de
>   Sunshine seemed like gold
> Since I cam North de
>   Whole damn world's turned cold.
> (quoted in Gates 1993:18)

The implications for women migrants were tremendous. Most were compelled to assume greater employment responsibilities in the Depression and war years, although the jobs available to them were typically limited to domestic and institutional service work. Historian Jacqueline Jones offers an apt summary of the limited opportunities African-American women faced in the 1930s: "Most of [the employed women] could find only seasonal or part-time employment; racial and sexual discrimination deprived them of a living wage no matter how hard they labored; and they endured a degree and type of workplace exploitation for which the mere fact of having a job could not compensate" (1985:199).

The women who moved to Philadelphia in the 1940s were not much better off. Even with the expanded economy during World War II, most African Americans were employed in domestic work positions; they could only watch as white women took the more lucrative and secure defense jobs. Most struggled as single mothers and described financial stability as a tenuous and fugitive goal. That, along with the sense of isolation from southern kin, made mothering a difficult and frightening experience. Yet in interview after interview the hardships, uncertainties and dilemmas of raising children under these conditions were mitigated by the sense of belonging and wisdom that their southern backgrounds and relations gave them; their southern experiences moored their mothering cultures even in the difficult and transformed social and economic framework they encountered in the North.

Migration and Medicalization:
The View from Upward Mobility

The medicalized cultures that migrant mothers developed in this new landscape were not monolithic, however, and we turn first to consider the story of a professional-class migrant family. Access to economic and social resources varied considerably among African-American migrants in Philadelphia. While most were working class or poor (and most moved between the two), a small number belonged to the upper middle class. One of these families, the Tanners, had a relationship to northern medical discourse that differed radically from that of the relatively poor migrant women who are the focus of the rest of this chapter. The Tanners' social and economic position, much like that of the middle-class Jewish families, allowed them to employ medicalization as a feature and sign of social mobility and their child care was self-consciously organized at a distance from southern remedies.[3]

Valerie and Henry Tanner migrated to Philadelphia as a married couple from a rural area in South Carolina in the 1920s. They began by working at jobs that were common for migrants: for a time, Valerie Tanner worked as a domestic. This was downward mobility: she was a college graduate and had been a teacher in the South. Henry Tanner took a number of jobs, among them working as a porter for a railroad, but eventually received a professional education and was able, after much hard work, to establish a successful mortuary business. The Tanners became leaders in the professional African-American community, which I discuss further in chapter 5.

I can provide some insight into their migration experience through the narrative of their daughter, Sue Thompson. It was in the context of her parents' social advance that Sue explained the medicalized culture her mother developed:

> My mother at that point . . . would have been considered a
> career woman. I mean, she was a career woman with, you know,
> the housekeeper and whatever. And she didn't do that ah,
> medical stuff to us, you know. She just would send us to the
> doctor. . . . And she was just that much ahead of [her time]. It
> was that you go to the doctor with things like that, that's all.

Valerie's lack of interest in traditional southern healing practices distinguished her from her sister, also a migrant. Sue explains:

> I mean, my aunt was, on the other hand, was a mender and a
> fixer-upper and a "Let's take care of it here" kind of person. [My
> mother] was of a different ilk in that, I say career [woman], I
> should have said, just advantaged, just above trying to do it
> herself. My mother used to tell me tales about what her mother
> used to do, but she couldn't remember what the stuff was. But
> my mother's sister, when I was there, and I was there often
> because in those days, a business was quarantined if you had
> any of the communicable diseases. And so whenever we would
> get measles, we had to go to [my aunt's house]. I picked up a
> case of ringworm in school, I have ringworm blotches all over
> my face and so she told my mother, "That's all right, I'll take
> her out there, I'll fix her." Well, it was the nastiest. It was so
> terrible, but I did it. She would put copper pennies in vinegar
> and then put that mess on my face, and it worked.

Yet for Valerie, being socially advanced made it necessary to repudiate the "mender" and "fixer-upper" mentality. Sue describes the stigma that was associated with the "asafetida bags," a traditional medicinal that many believed could "keep away" illness (Snow 1993). The bags, worn around the neck, contain a resinous, foul-smelling material derived from the roots of plants:

> I think, and that may be a piece that you need here, I think
> that there is some stigma attached to the home remedies.
> Because the asafetida bags, I mean we used to laugh at the kids
> that wore them, you know. . . . And yet they were well children
> and I mean, they would stink to high heaven, but they didn't
> get sick, you hear. They did not get sick.

Sue presented the home remedies as medically effective but socially inappropriate, as though both the labor of performing home remedies and the local knowledge they relied on were out of place in her mother's new social milieu; expert discourse represented the style and symbol of social advancement. What DeVault says about how professional and managerial women use cooking discourse pertains here as well: "Through education and participation in class-related activities . . . wives learn to take expert instruction about everyday life quite seriously and to attend to the details of elaborated ideals for household practices" (1991:218). Indeed, by evaluating home remedies in relation to social position, Valerie participated in the new culture of medicalization that posed scientific medicine in contrast to traditional methods of health care as a difference between present and past. But rather than view home remedies as backward or primitive, as did the Jewish women, Sue's parents permitted the continued use of traditional practices. In creating her professional and advanced household, Valerie appeared to view herself as modern and advantaged while continuing to sanction the traditional remedies her sister knew. This was a model of medicalization unlike the exclusive model developed by the Jewish women; Valerie embraced medical discourse as a status marker but did not distinguish it as the exclusive field of relevance (Hall 1992).

Sue's identification of the "stigma attached to home remedies" speaks to this point. Indeed, home remedies were stigmatized precisely because they signaled social marginality—poverty, social exclusion, or poor judgment (Fraser 1998). Allowing the use of home remedies in this upwardly mobile African-American family—or admitting of their use to me—was something that Sue and Valerie perceived as shameful, as violating their new respectability.

The level of control and the range of healing alternatives open to the Tanner family were not typical among the African-American women I interviewed. The vast majority of migrants did not enjoy the economic and social luxuries of the Tanner household. Although the migrants moved to Philadelphia with hopes of achieving more secure economic lives, migration did not usher them into the northern world of opportunity and economic advance. Reports of dislocation dominate. To understand their perceptions of displacement and their distance from medical discourse, it is necessary to see how these women defined mothering in the South, which gave them a yardstick with which to measure their new mothering situation in Philadelphia.

Mothering in the South

Phyllis Taylor, though she moved from a North Carolina farm as a teenager and raised all her children in Philadelphia, shows the signifi-

cance African-American mothers gave to their connections to southern kin:

> I never forget, once I took my baby home. I went down and she
> was a year old and wasn't walking. And oh man, I was one of
> those mothers. The children was always kept spotless. My
> aunt'd say, "You let that child get out there and get dirty, she'll
> walk." She said, "You don't wanna bathe and clean up, I'll do
> it." So I let Lorraine get out there and crawl in the mud, wet
> herself, you know, in the mud and crawl in it. And bless her,
> when I brought her back here she was walking. Now I don't
> know whether that really did it or not. Maybe she was gonna
> walk anyway, huh. . . . And I happened to go home. Now I
> didn't take her down there for that, I don't think that actually
> did it. I think there was a lot of children around and by her
> being out there you know, and wanting to keep up with them it
> might have helped her get more of a push or more willpower.

Phyllis was one of the few working-class African-American women who
believed that "going to a physician was part of being a good mother."
Nonetheless, whether it was her aunt's intervention or the motivation
provided by the other children, Phyllis's story gives obvious value to
the care-taking knowledge and power of kin relations in the South. The
South was considered home by virtually all of the women I interviewed,
and although many were frustrated by the racism and poverty that characterized the South, they loved it for the healing and caring they found
there, a perception that, according to anthropologist Carol Stack
(1996), partially explains the return migration to the South of many
African Americans in the late twentieth century.

In the accounts of the women I interviewed, motherhood in the
South is characterized by community and kin networks. Motherhood
and child care practices are treated in their narratives not as an individual undertaking but as the responsibility of the community. Moreover, direct experience with child care, rather than abstract learning
or the formal knowledge and practices of medical discourse, is understood as the basis for mothers' knowledge.

The women I interviewed mentioned almost no contact with physicians or nurses in the South. The reasons for their silence about contact with medical professionals reflect the racial divides in the South;

they reflect the reality that medical care was to a great extent unavailable to blacks who were geographically isolated in southern rural regions. The health status of African Americans in the South prior to World War II was virtually as endangered as during slavery (Beardsley 1987). Death from tuberculosis and heart disease and during childbirth and infancy accounted for short life expectancy. African Americans also had very high morbidity rates compared to whites.

Part of the racial difference in morbidity and mortality was attributable to the inferior daily living conditions that poor southern African Americans experienced: overcrowded housing, lack of sanitary facilities and clean water, poverty, and malnutrition. In his study of health care for African Americans before 1950 in Georgia and South and North Carolina, Edward Beardsley concludes that risk factors for poor health such as poor sanitary facilities, low levels of education, malnutrition, and high stress were "heightened" for blacks:

> For blacks, especially those in the South, racism and institutionalized segregation heightened the effect of every other variable. America's health and medical professions and its political leadership groped very slowly toward an understanding of the economic, social, and cultural parameters of health. They moved even more haltingly in developing the will to change the system of life that bound blacks to their fate of ill health and early death. (1987:28)

Medical treatment was virtually unavailable to rural southern African Americans: There was a severe shortage of hospital bed space for African Americans; most of the black hospitals were located in cities, which few blacks had access to; and there were very few black physicians. Furthermore, many white physicians continued to believe in the biological inferiority of African Americans—and took little interest in treating them.

Nor did the public health establishment do much to fill the gap. The concern with public health in the South emerged in the early twentieth century when doctors, local social reformers, and African-American leaders began to identify the poor health status of vulnerable populations. Until the infusion of federal money during the New Deal era, southern public health leaders did little to address the health needs of African Americans (Beardsley 1987; Fraser 1998). Before then, public health care in the South, according to Fraser, progressed through "fits and starts" (1998:32) and African Americans hardly benefited from the limited services they provided (Beardsley 1987).

The regulation of African-American midwives that was part of the public health initiative had direct relevance for mothers. Beginning at the turn of the century, African-American midwives were slowly but surely forced out of reproductive health care. In part because lay midwives created some occupational competition with physicians, in part because they did not represent the new, modern science, and in part because they were not white, African-American midwives were portrayed by many white private physicians and public health practitioners as dangerous and as contributing to the high maternal death rates (Fraser 1998; Ladd-Taylor 1994). Monitoring lay midwives, curtailing their authority, and stigmatizing their patients came to define much of southern public health work through the 1940s.

Yet among the women I interviewed, it was the "midwoman," or "midwife," who was the principal medical figure they recalled from the South. Given midwives' distance from and conflict with the formal medical establishment, a woman who consulted a midwife was not likely to take on medicalized activities, as did women who gave birth in hospitals or with attending physicians (Leavitt 1986; Fraser 1998). Indeed, women's use of midwives defined mothers as outside the periphery of medicine.

Mildred James, who raised her three children in North Carolina before moving to Philadelphia with them, points to the distance of the doctor in her description of the midwife's duties:

> And I know everything is different now than it was when I was raising my kids. Because now, everything they do, they go to get a statement from the doctor. But when I was raising mine, I didn't get no statement from no doctor. 'Cause it wasn't no doctor in the country, but a midwoman. . . . You didn't go to the hospital to have a baby. You just get the midwife to come and deliver the baby and clean you up and go home and then come back [in] a couple of days and see how the baby doing, and then that's that. You's on your own.

THE SIGNIFICANCE OF COMMUNITY

On an everyday basis, Mildred was immersed in caretaking relations with community members and kin on whom she relied for advice and support. The knowledge she generated from these relations were an alternative to the doctor's, as she explains:

> Why go to the doctor and ask them everything? You got a mind of your own. . . . I mean, you have to use your own judgment sometime about your own kids. You feel better to ask your mother and then as she said, "What I don't know, you go to the doctor, or ask somebody else." Then you feel like [asking] somebody in neighborhood, you know, [who] had more kids, instead—they had more children than my mother did 'cause my mother didn't have but me. And if somebody had about three or four more kids, they know a little bit more than what my mother knew because they had more kids than she did.

For Mildred, "neighborhood" ties provided the basis for mothering knowledge and practice and offered a grounding for her identity as a mother. Mildred explains:

> Look. When I was raising my kids I was in the country, you couldn't run to the doctor, you know, every time they get sick. You just give 'em, I used to give 'em Castoria. The older people would tell me, you know. They'll tell you what to go and get, you know, and help doctor 'em.

Mildred situates herself as part of this ongoing community, as subject to its understandings, and as dependent on its help.

Mary Herbert's ideas about community caretaking illustrate this theme. As a mother in Savannah, Georgia, she rarely consulted or even encountered medical personnel. I asked Mary whether she took her daughter for a checkup in Savannah. She responded with an answer that had little to do with medicine and everything to do with community:

> I didn't go in for a checkup down there, people in the neighborhood, you know—see down there it's different from up here. . . . If you live in a neighborhood down there, everybody call you family. You know, they look out for you. If they see you doing something, the children doing something they're not supposed to do, they chastise them, you know. And then they tell your

mother and you come and your mother do the same thing.
Everybody know each other. You live in a neighborhood a long
time, you know everybody.

For Mary, the checkup extended beyond the narrow medical-technical
meaning I had in mind when I questioned her; the neighbors were caretakers and provided the focus of her mothering practices. Mary discusses
"checking up" in a broader sense than checking height, weight, and
feeding and sleeping patterns. The "checkup" extended to monitoring
behavior and assuring safety, resources that the community could offer
but that a physician could not. Both Mary and Mildred conceive of caretaking along ties of familiarity with and trust in individuals with whom
they share values and life experiences.

Given the racially segregated and racist nature of the South and
the dominance of whites in medical-care delivery, African-American
women's distance from medicine was also based on a racial distance
(Beardsley 1987; Grant 1998). In health, as in other activities, women's
lives in the South were characterized by extreme racial segregation. Lucy
Alston, born in North Carolina in 1909, tells of living within and validating a racially homogenous context for caretaking:

> You didn't have to go to the white people for what you wanted
> to know, because if you had a mother or aunt or some of your
> [people] . . . I remember when I was about fourteen years old [in
> North Carolina], my mother was sick over a year and my aunt
> was taking care of her. I got sick. I think they still call it the
> yellow jaundice. . . . [An] old lady came by while we was out
> washing, out in the yard, and my eyes was yellow. So, she said
> to my aunt, "That child got the yellow jaundice. . . . Get you
> some peach tree leaves and make a tea." Now I don't know, I
> can't remember whether any doctor give me any medicine or
> not, but I do know that's what cleared it up. And I haven't had
> no problem since.

Lucy marginalizes medicine, specifically the medicine of white people,
by invoking the knowledge and guardianship of community and kin:
the doctor, the white outsider, remains on the periphery as she vali-
dates the traditional remedy over the expert's and women's everyday
caretaking over formal medical intervention. She created a boundary

around her racial community, one that created a zone of safety for her at the same time as it kept strangers, in this case the white doctor, out.

Thus, in women's descriptions of motherhood in the South we find an emphasis on community and kin caretaking and an immersion in established and trusted practices. These relations and practices provided the ingredients for safety and protection. Mothering was not a site that women used to distinguish themselves from the identities of elders or other community members. Instead, these women spoke of mothering as an arena for enacting allegiance to community and kinship ties and saw themselves as protected by them.

THE SIGNIFICANCE OF EXPERIENCE

All I learned I learned from my mother. And I learned
how to live from my mother.

                                        Brenda Sheppard

Brenda Sheppard, the mother of fourteen children, celebrates her mother's life as the basis for her own. For Brenda, as for the other southern mothers, it was the knowledge gained by experience—by life, in other words—that provided the foundation for her own. Shirley Elliot, who raised her first child for a year in North Carolina, explains that it was by continuing her mother's practices that she was able to provide the context for her children's health:

> 'Cause [I raised them] the way my mother brought us up. Along
> in the South, you know, that's the way the people brought the
> children up. You ain't hear talk about sickness around the
> children.

Homegrown food, warm clothing, and moral upbringing were understood as the basis for children's health. This separate belief system helped to define community consensus and boundaries, and kept other health systems at bay. These health beliefs were connected to African medical lore, which holds that illness results from an individual's failure to maintain bodily or spiritual harmony. "Natural illness" is understood to come from an imbalance in the physical system, particularly an imbalance of intake and outgo, which can be corrected with teas, roots, and herbal preparations. Shirley recalls the cleansing effect of sassafras tea:

In the spring [down South], we would drink that sassafras tea.
That would be our tea. And in the fall that would be our tea.
And that would keep your blood, cleanse your blood.

"Unnatural illnesses," coming from the evil acts of others (caused by emotions such as jealousy or anger) or by an individual's inability to deal with life's stresses, are addressed through charms, rituals, and incantations. These African beliefs were combined with many Native American remedies, European medical practices, the available material resources, and the exigencies of everyday life to become the healing system adhered to by many African-American southerners (Fraser 1998; Lemke-Santangelo 1996; Snow 1993).

Brenda and Shirley also trust and revere the lessons learned from direct experience. This orientation differs from that of the dominant paradigm in which knowledge is subject to critique and analysis, ideally independent of the influences of values, social positions, and knowers (Harding 1986). For the African-American women respondents, knowledge is rooted in connection not distance, an orientation described by Patricia Hill Collins: "These forms of knowledge allow for subjectivity between the knower and the known, rest in the women themselves (not in higher authorities), and are experienced directly in the world (not through abstraction)" (1990:211). Of course, the upwardly mobile Jewish and African-American women who validated modern medical knowledge did not in any way test this knowledge for its empirical accuracy. Their belief in the superiority of medical discourse over immigrant's practice was an artifact of their status negotiation as much as it was an embrace of formal scientific principals. Yet for these African-American women, whose motherhood practices were not fashioned to represent upward mobility, experiential knowledge held value as a body of information, an expression of identity, and a symbol of group membership. These women were oriented toward the knowledge, values, and traditions of trusted individuals and in their practices they supported not a fracture between generations but a continuing process of weaving the generations together.

Women's descriptions of traditional knowledge and home remedies during our interviews offer excellent examples of how this epistemological orientation reflected women's ties to their communities. They described these practices with a vividness and level of detail that was remarkable. Unlike the Jewish women, whose stories about remedies were vague and diffuse, these women told numerous stories about home remedies, had an awareness of what these remedies were used for and how they worked, and often knew when to use them. My own reactions to women's descriptions of home remedies provides another kind of gauge about the different meaning of traditional practice in their lives. I found myself chuckling along with the Jewish women about the silliness of the various home remedies: in the context of their lives as modern women, the remedies seem silly, irrelevant, a relic of a dangerous and backward past. Admitting to using these remedies would point essentially to inadequate mothering, to the use of outdated and inferior mothering practices.

But never once in my conversations with the African-American women was I inclined to laugh or to see these remedies as silly. Rather, I found comfort in their descriptions. Some women closed their eyes as if they were re-creating a scene in their minds, others gave long and finely detailed accounts. Indeed, this kind of expression is particularly interesting, given the stigma that was associated with traditional remedies. It may be the case that the expansive and sympathetic portraits of home remedies served for these women as a shield against the judgment of outsiders like me, and that these descriptions functioned to keep dominant medicine on the margin during the interviews themselves.

Clara Franks, who was born in North Carolina and raised her children in Philadelphia, never forgot the healing dimensions and personal connections provided by such traditional practice:

> My grandmother kept a piece of flannel she washed, baked, and rolled up in paper with string around it. She'd put it in the oven and bake it. Then she'd roll it up. Uh hum, that was sterilizing it. And she would grease my chest with beef suet. She'd mix it with a little camphorated oil. And she'd rub it on my chest and then she'd put the other shirt on with the long sleeves and the flannel nightgown. Oh, I have a good sweat from it, you know. And I was ready to go to school the next day. 'Cause I loved school. I didn't want to miss.

I asked Clara how this felt.

> It felt so comforting. Then she would, had a piece of sheep's wool . . . to put at the bottom of my bed. To keep it warm 'cause

we didn't have heat, we had a fireplace. And she would heat a brick and iron and roll it up in the material and an old blanket and put the sheep's skin over it. And it kept my feet warm. You know the things that she [did], oh, she was a beautiful grandmother.

The idea that her grandmother's knowledge and practice offered healing properties challenges the dominant medical view that health knowledge is the possession of a small number of specially trained individuals. Clara's belief in the efficacy and significance of these traditional practices, embedded as they were in her daily kin relations, reflected an epistemology where it was direct experience and connection between individuals that offered the basis for healing.

The validation of experience was rooted also in the organization of family and caretaking that these women experienced in the South. Unlike in the nuclear-family pattern validated in medical discourse, in Jewish women's narratives, and more generally in the dominant culture, each of these migrant women grew up in households where neighbors cared for each other and where multiple generations performed household work together. The ten women who began to raise their children in the South did so in these extended household forms, where the lines between generations and households were blurred and where caretaking was defined as a collective effort.

The collective organization of caretaking encouraged learning from elders. Living with grandparents or next to well-known neighbors meant that these women were themselves treated with traditional remedies, an experience that taught them to value experiential knowledge and the efficacy of traditional practices (Blake 1977; Snow 1993). The collective form of caretaking also meant that as children, most of these women held extensive household responsibilities of their own. Work was so central a feature of their daily lives and so much the basis for their understanding of mothering that when I asked Brenda what she wished for when she was a little girl, she responded by saying, "We didn't have time for that" and went on to tell me about the farmwork, schoolwork, and housework, from "sunup to sundown," that she undertook from a very young age.

It was through their participation in these activities that these women learned much about child care and mothering. When I asked

Shirley how she learned to be a mother she stressed the importance of her own experience:

> Oh, I don't know much about learning, but you know, just
> seeing how, you know, how [Mother] fed them and changing
> them, you know. Just watching. 'Cause you know, mothers back
> there, they didn't, you know, take time to tell you. I don't
> know. I just learned it. I guess, doing [it]. . . . Some of my little
> brothers and sisters, you know, they were babies under me. And
> see, I learned. See how my mother would do, and you know, we
> would have to help take care of them.

Shirley refers to a model of teaching that is not focused on formal learning, where one listens, watches, and absorbs new information, but one rooted in doing the activities to be learned. Ruth explains that this process of doing the work gave her the knowledge she needed to raise her children:

> My mother laid the pattern out for you to grow by. That was
> knowing how to take care of your children. My mother was
> around all, most of the time when I was growing up. So I
> learned a lot from her. And she, she would tell you what to do
> and what not to do. I used to take care of the childrens. Like
> when she had children, I used to do a lot of taking care of
> them. So I learned a lot by that.

Mildred described a similar lesson and experience:

> [My mother] was with me all the time. Well, she taught me how
> to clean, cook, she taught me how to cook. She taught me
> how to clean. She taught me how to wash. I was cooking when
> I was, uh, about ten years old. 'Cause my mother was sick. She
> couldn't. And so I had to, she taught me how to cook. I was so
> small, I had to stand up on her stool and make bread. But she
> always would make me wash my hands, clean my nails out.
> After I cleaned my nails out, then I had to wash my hands
> again. Then's I'd make the bread.

Thus, it was in the context of their everyday participation in extended relations of caretaking that these women report having received the lessons of mothering. Learning about mothering was not a discrete activity detached from the daily round of relationships and obligations to others, but one that emerged within and helped to define them. Suzanne Carothers discusses the significance of domestic work for African-American households: "Black domestic units are centered around the needs and work of the household. Because of the necessity of so much work . . . working together has become one of the major vehicles for learning. Learning is made attractive in this context because it represents access to adulthood and to continued membership in the family and community" (1990:242). Having experience with child care and domestic work as children, witnessing the necessity and value given to traditional remedies, and connecting oneself to a community of caretakers focused the meaning of motherhood for these southern women.

Women's collectively based caretaking, experiential knowledge, and distance from expert discourse resonates with themes found in African-American women's literature. Literary critic Valerie Lee asserts that African-American women writers such as Zora Neale Hurston, Toni Cade Bambara, Toni Morrison, Alice Walker, and Gloria Naylor construct characters who are medical men, anthropologists, and other experts as symbols of power and control, as threats to the knowledge that communities establish, and as violations of African-Americans' privacy and bodily integrity. In African-American women's writing, experts are portrayed as commodifying black women's bodies, treating them like they do other "texts" on which they symbolize their power. By criticizing notions of objectivity and principles of empiricism as culturally biased and dangerous, African-American women writers craft an oppositional discourse in which concrete experience, faith, caretaking, and dialogue provide the basis for knowledge. Writing in this tradition celebrates "subjugated forms of knowledge," according to Lee: "Although not having the type of power that is predicated upon white Western masculinist ideology, they bring with them alternative conceptions of both power and knowledge" (1996:67). For the women in my study, forging an "alternative conception" to dominant forms of power took place among community and kin. It meant validating a knowledge system that was increasingly stigmatized and suspect, and valuing the everyday actions toward child health that were embedded in community relations. Moving to the North threatened these patterns and opened migrants up to the dangers, control, and neglect of organized medicine.

Narratives of Migration, Narratives of Dislocation

The migration experience for these women contrasts with those of the Jewish women I interviewed and Valerie Tanner's, in which distance from elders and the embrace of and adaptability to new knowledge constituted the framework for mothering practice and identity. Economically mobile and socially ambitious, these mothers constructed new relations of caretaking organized around expert discourse. The working-class and working-poor African-American migrant women, by contrast, continued to affirm the practices of their past, even—or especially—as they faced a new and changed landscape for motherhood.

As much as the migration North reflected the desire and occasionally the reality of a better life, migrant mothers were confronted with tremendous disruption in their mothering practices. They moved out of the insulating and protective circle of community and kin. Not surprisingly, migrant women indicated a continuing attachment to the South. This is a preference that has been noted by scholars of migration (Clark-Lewis 1994; Hine 1996; Lemke-Santangelo 1996; Marks 1989). In her analysis of women's migration to the Midwest, Darlene Clark Hine asserts that many women, having left a child and other family at home, maintained continuing interdependencies with family members in the South and helped to bring southern culture to the North. Most migrant women, she argues, developed only "incomplete ties" to the North: "Unable to or unwilling to sever ties to or abandon irrevocably the South, black women's assimilation to urban life remained fragmented and incomplete" (1996:250).

Gretchen Lemke-Santangelo's study of migrants to the Pacific Northwest adds that southernness was a "highly fluid concept" (1996:135). The practices, values, and styles of migrants' everyday lives—ones they attributed to the South—were created and interpreted to fit the resources in the North. "What remained," according to Lemke-Santangelo, was the "perception of something as solidly 'Southern'" (1996:135). Whether migrant culture remained or ever was actually southern is immaterial, according to Lemke-Santangelo. What does matter is that migrants considered themselves, their homes, and their practices as "solidly 'Southern,'" an orientation that not only provided the knowledge essential for mothering but also enacted one's group membership and obligations in what often felt like a hostile and unwelcoming environment.

Three case studies elaborate the dominant themes that the migrant women raised when describing this transformation of mothering: dangers in the North, the exposure to but continuing irrelevance of medicine for daily practice, and the re-establishment of southern ties and practices in Philadelphia. For Reather Herbert, migration meant a more dangerous health context. (See chapter 5 for an examination of the black health movement in Philadelphia.)

REATHER HERBERT: THE DANGEROUS NORTH

Reather Herbert experienced the transition to Philadelphia as an encounter with daily health practices that she considered more dangerous than those followed in the South. As a young girl in Greenville, Reather did farm work to help her sharecropping family as well as paid domestic work for the owner of the land. She lived with her mother, stepfather, and siblings, who helped raise her children. Reather reports having had no contact with doctors throughout her time in the South. Instead, illness was managed by her stepfather:

> We didn't go to the doctor's. My stepfather, he didn't take
> nobody to the doctor's. We would get those cobwebs and put
> them over [a cut] to stop the bleeding. He would wrap it
> himself. . . . You get it in a ball, kind of like hair you take out in
> a comb. Well you just put it on that place that was real bad [to]
> stop it from bleeding. And we didn't have no doctor then. We
> got sick with a cold he gave you three-sixes. It's some kind of
> medicine. It's real liver. And . . . if there were small children he
> would give them castor oil. He just didn't believe in doctors.
> He make his own medicine. Go in the woods. He'd be gone
> practically all day long. And he come back with the roots and
> herbs and fix up whatever he want to fix.

In her description of how baby food was produced and used in the South we also see an immersion in tradition and in kin caretaking:

> My mother have my oldest children, they would be eatin' and
> she would, ah, like she was eating, she would chew up food in
> her mouth and then take it and put it in the baby's mouth.

That's the way old people use to feed the baby. Whatever they
was eating. If it was meat and bread or molasses or collard
greens or whatever. They would eat it and then take so much
out of their mouth and put it in the baby's mouth. That's the
way the older children were fed.

The local production of food also represented a link to the community and to elders and was an occasion on which she both learned
and used the valued knowledge they passed on. It was the loss of this
social context that made feeding up North so dangerous.

Moving to Philadelphia meant a new context of work: Reather was
employed in a factory as a trimmer, did part-time domestic work, and
lived with her sister. With migration, Reather entered a new context
of caring relations, one that meant she too, like other migrants, had to
resort to practices, people, and services that went beyond her immediate and trusted social network. An overriding sense that the North presented a more dangerous, less healthful place for children dominates
Reather's narrative, as, for example, in her description of childbirth at
the beginning of this chapter. She focuses also on the new dangers of
food and feeding wrought by the northern context where strangers,
rather than family and community, produce food:

Now so many people get sick up here. All that stuff they spray
on them collards. And when you buy the collards they's already
cut up and everything. You don't know how the collards was
washed. . . . But see, we were washing 'em. See my mother . . .
had these big tubs down there. She would put the collards in
there and wash the tub out and put a whole [lot] in there and
put baking soda in there. And you wash the collards like that.

Reather's fear of purchased foods speaks to her sense of dislocation from
her relations of caring at home. In her study of food and cultural identity among the Gullah, Josephine Beoku-Betts also found a direct link
between concern about store-bought foods and the disruption to traditional practices and social relations brought by modernization. One of
her informants, Anne Willis, explains this problem in terms much like
Reather's:

When I was a child coming up, we never used to put fertilizer
in our crop to rush up the food. Food used to taste much better

then than now. The old folks didn't have as many health
problem as we are having and they ate all those forbidden
foods. I think it's the fertilizers and chemicals they put in the
food now. Seem to me that children were more healthy in those
days than they are now. (1995:548)

According to Reather, similarly, migration disrupted the social relations
of feeding and other caretaking as much as it changed the food itself.

JAMIE RIVERS: THE IRRELEVANCE OF MEDICINE

Jamie Rivers's narrative illustrates how far the presumptions of medical
discourse were from her daily life. She was born in 1916 in Lewisberg,
North Carolina. She grew up on a farm and attended school up to the
fifth grade. She was fourteen when she had her first child, and went
on to have seven more, three in the South and four in Philadelphia,
one of whom died as a young child from meningitis. While in Lewisberg,
Jamie lived with her mother, her husband, and her children. Jamie's
husband went up North to Philadelphia, got a job in an industrial plant,
and sent for the family. In 1944 Jamie, with four children, moved North.
A number of Jamie's siblings were already there, and they helped establish the recent migrants. Jamie was a housekeeper for a Philadelphia
newspaper company for years, working from four P.M. until midnight.
Like other migrant women of her social class, Jamie had very little contact with modern medicine in the South:

> Ain't no nurses been to my, our, house when we was, when I
> was in North Carolina. When I found out all this [doctors]
> what I know now is since I came to Philadelphia. Yeah. Yes
> ma'am. Yes ma'am. But down in North Carolina we don't have
> all that down there. Not runnin' to doctors.

Jamie's report on the only occasion in which a physician entered her
house as a child is revealing in this context. She remembers him as a
white man who endangered her mother's life:

> My mother had a canker on the back of her neck. It [was] like a
> ball in the back of her neck. And they kept messing with it and
> shouldn't have been messin' with it, with a pin [because] they
> turn it into a cancer. They pick it, you know. And then see
> that, I don't think the pin was sterilized and it turned to that.

Jamie's contention that the doctor created the "cancer" through care-lessness articulates the lack of trust and sense of vulnerability she felt in the face of these strange and distant professionals. Dominant medi-cine represented interference from the outside, not a desired or benevo-lent medical intervention.

For her routine mothering in Philadelphia, Jamie remained deeply suspicious of the formal knowledge of modern medicine, even though her encounters with it expanded greatly. She delivered her babies in the hospital, in contrast to the North Carolina home births in which she relied on an African-American midwife secured and paid for by her mother. Only on rare occasions did she consult the city's clinic, explain-ing that "you got to have money to go to the [clinic]" and then only when the children were sick with something she herself could not handle. Her narrative shows medicine from the perspective of some-one who has little control over it:

> I don't know what [the doctors] did but if they get sick we'll take them there. And they say, Miss Rivers or Mr. Rivers, you do so and so. So, don't let her or don't let him have so and so.

In contrast to her vague recollection of the physician's remedies, Jamie is quick to recollect and reveal the importance and usefulness of the home remedy of castor oil. Jamie trusted traditional remedies, as the following quote indicates: "I used [something] that they don't believe in up here. Like if one of them get sick with a cold I give castor oil to get the cold out of you." I asked Jamie where she had heard of castor oil:

> From down South. That's where. That's my home. I give castor oil for getting the cold out of your stomach. I didn't know about no extra Tylenol and things 'til I come to Philadelphia.[4]

Jamie's assertion that "home" is the source of knowledge signals that social relations—not formal expertise or abstract knowledge—provide the basis for expertise. And by opposing her valued home to Philadel-phia's "extra Tylenol," Jamie also acknowledges that time, space, and place organize the available options and the desirable strategies for child health. Here we find neither the imperatives we heard from middle- and upper-middle-class women (e.g., "I had to use doctors") nor a belief that knowledge advances in a linear progression (e.g., "Doctors have better knowledge").

Jamie's distance from the dominant medical establishment is apparent in her belief that she had the knowledge necessary for mothering, even though the hospital's outreach efforts presumed she did not:

> Nowadays in the hospital they try to show you how to take care. But if you alone, by yourself, and you had the baby, it would come to you. You wouldn't need nobody coming. Even if you go to the hospital and they say, "I'm gonna send a nurse." You do it yourself. It will come to you. How to treat your baby and what to do for your baby and how to feed your baby and you don't need no teachin' on it. No ma'am, don't need no teachin' on it.

It was Jamie's mother who provided her education:

> My mother just told me what to do. She said, Jim, she said, "Don't never fix your baby a bottle unless you sterilize that bottle. Sterilize that bottle good. And then after you sterilize that bottle and then you put your formula in there for that baby if you're gonna give 'em a little cereal now, nothing but pure milk, or out of the can." Anyway, she said, "But right before you got to sterilize these bottles, very, very, very good [before] you give him any, anything in this bottle." And after you know that one time you don't need no more help. You don't need no more help. You don't need nothing else. You know what to do.

Jamie's reverence for her mothers' lessons continued, even in the face of the radically changed circumstances of her mothering. Jamie's orientation, while it borrowed the public health idea of "sterilization," was organized to keep dominant medicine at the border of her mother work. In trusting her mother as the source of knowledge about baby feeding, Jamie invokes a sustained connection to the women's culture of her community and constructs her continuing ties to "home."

MARY HERBERT: MAKING NEW CONNECTIONS

Mary Herbert, having grown up in Savannah, spent the first five years of mothering living with many of her twelve siblings, who helped raise her baby daughter. Mary was thirteen years old when she had her baby.

Her mother died when the baby was nine months old. At that point, Mary began paid domestic work for a neighboring white family, a job she took over from her mother. It was from this employer that Mary learned early on about the modern products of baby care:

> We were very, very poor, you know. And my mother used to work [domestic work] for a lady and she used to send Mom all kind of baby food. [The baby] never like it. I didn't know why she wouldn't eat it but she didn't eat it. They thought [it was] good for the baby and she send it to me. I thought it was very nice. But Gloria wouldn't eat it. It was another lady lived in my neighborhood. She had a lot of children and she was stuck and I gave it to her. And they ate it, she fixed it, and they ate it.

In her study of African-American domestic workers' relations to their white employers, Bonnie Thornton Dill (1994) found that domestic workers often adopt symbols of their employers' upward mobility when these seem advantageous for their own children (we will see examples of that in chapter 6). But Mary invokes her distance. Indeed, her description of the "rich, white family" for whom she worked reflects the disparity between her own life and theirs, a disparity that may have made their baby food irrelevant:

> I nursed [the baby] for two years. She never ate baby food. I nursed her and gave her food from the table. [She ate] the same kind of food I would eat myself. . . . Everything is different now than it was back there. Well, you know, certain formulas and things you have to feed these kids. Well, when I was coming up, people who was poor didn't have the money to buy that kind of stuff. So whatever you could feed them, you mash it up or whatever, you know, and fed it to them.

Mary moved out of her network of caretaking relations in 1947, when she went to Philadelphia as an eighteen-year-old mother. She understands her migration experience as defined largely through her accommodation to the new work environment:

> When I first came here, um, I wanted to go back, you know. You know, everything was different. You didn't know nobody and I got here at night and the next morning I looked around and [thought about] going back home. And my sister had

gotten me this job where I first started working. And I sat
down, they tried to learn me how to do the work. And I
couldn't do it and I'd get up, grab my stuff, you know, my lunch
bag and my pocketbook and I'd get up and I'd say, "Look, I got,
I'm here. I've got to learn. I've got to learn how to do it. You
know, I'm not going to get disgusted, you know, because I've
never learned." So I finally, finally, um, learned how to do the
work and as long as I knew how to do the work I was fine. I
worked every day [and] during the weekend I did cleaning and
go back to work again [on Monday].

Mary initially moved in with her sister. In 1948 she married another
migrant from the South and they moved to their own apartment. Mary
did not have any other children and divorced in 1952.

Mary developed a close relationship with her neighbor Patricia, who
knew Mary's husband from the South. "He knew her and he said she's
a real nice person, and she was," Mary says. Patricia became Mary's primary support for child care, and their tie was legitimated and maintained through their common southern backgrounds. "She was just like
family member. We all just were like one big family. Whatever we had
we shared together." Patricia took the role of the knowledgeable elder
in the caretaking community that Mary had left behind:

Well, she had children of her own and I saw how she treated
her children, my daughter just like she was one of hers, you
know. . . . I was fairly young, so she knew a little bit more than I
did. But she treated her just like she was one of hers. She did.
She would talk to me, you know, about different things and like
when I came up here I didn't know anybody, you know. And
she just would talk to me like a mom. Like your mom would
talk to you about different things.

Other migrant women also cultivated relations with women and men
from the South, often but not always family members (Lemke-
Santangelo 1996). The establishment of extended relations of caretaking such as they had had in the South went a long way toward validating
southern health practices, as Mary explains:

She used to use home remedies with her children. Yes. A lot of
people that come from the South, a lot of mothers, really know

about home remedies, especially older people, you know. And
sometimes their children will take it on from them and do the
same thing.

Mary developed a new caretaking culture within the context of the familiarity of southern practices. Hers was not an approach that con-
sciously pulled against the collective and traditional orientation of the
practices she had valued in the South, but that integrated them into
her new social position in the North.

This chapter has shown motherhood from the perspective of women
who developed fragile ties to the dominant medical forms and codes of
motherhood. I have argued that their motherhood practices were forged
within a context of social marginality, in both the South and the North.
Facing racism, isolation, and lack of economic opportunity in both geographic regions, these women worked to develop mothering practices
that empowered their local knowledge, took advantage of local opportunity, and offered a basis for assurance. While in Philadelphia they were
increasingly confronted with organized medicine, they continued to
forge a model of motherhood that was at a distance from dominant
medical forms.

The promise of medical discourse to elevate women's social acceptability held only for some women. Indeed, dominant medicine's promise could not be one of a shared and universally accessible social code.
Because women's relations to medical discourse were structured by identity and position, it is necessary to conceive of medicalization as a cultural and social phenomenon that is inseparable from questions of
insider and outsider, inclusion and exclusion, and about American society and women's place within it. Indeed, medicalization prompted
women to reflect on their social position and, in doing so, maintain
and express their commonality with some women and difference from
others. It is to understanding that process that the book now turns.

Women's Networks, Divided Motherhood, and the Legitimation of Medical Authority

Part II

Chapter 4

"The Doctor Was Just Like One of Us"

Insiders, Outsiders, and Jewish Women's Medicalized Mothering

At a family gathering a few years ago, I was describing the home remedies that African-American women told me they had used to help their sick babies when my cousin Bessie suddenly remarked, "They don't know why they're doing it—it's tribal." I start this section of the book on women's networks and differences among women with this unfortunate, and for my cousin, uncharacteristic remark, because I think it highlights how medical discourse has become involved in the cultural production of motherhood in this century. What personal and cultural distance from "tribalness" does Bessie assume about her own mothering techniques? What makes her believe that the remedies that she gleaned from medical authorities, on whom she relied in raising her own children, advanced and superior? And on what basis and with what authority does Bessie make such judgments?

The case studies in part 1 on migrancy, identity, and medicalization show mothers evaluating medical discourse as an element of their own status work. The narratives point to the multiple and contradictory meanings of medical discourse from their diverse perspectives, showing that the discourse was not culturally neutral but entailed social mobility for some and marginality and dislocation for others. Moreover, it was not only in relation to their private domestic units that the women's mothering culture was established. Mothers engaged and produced their medicalized cultures in the context of social networks of other women.

It has been typical in the social science literature on the family to presume that it is primarily among poor families that extrafamilial networks assume significance for mothering. These relations have been seen as temporary at best, aberrant at worst, departing from the pattern of the idealized nuclear family. And, in medical writing, these networks have been denigrated, considered the source of "superstition" and targeted as the location where threats to medical authority are generated (Litt 1993). Yet the women I spoke with gave very different impressions of the importance and meaning of their networks for their mothering. All the women, from the poorest to the wealthiest, developed extensive networks that they considered essential to their child care, although the forms and material bases of these ties differed. Moreover, there was no simple formula that equated women's networks with a challenge to medical authority. Rather, I found a complicated and shifting web of relations to medical discourse, where women's networks enabled both distance from and access to dominant medicine, although how these relations functioned varied. It became clear, finally, that it was women's work to maintain their households' connection to these social networks and to mitigate the pressures and carry out the obligations that they raised. Rather than provide a vague backdrop within which, or against which, women develop medicalized mothering cultures, these networks figured in women's narratives as a daily feature of caretaking that secured children's health and mothers' styles of parenting.

Furthermore, women's network relations and obligations are vitally engaged in the creation and maintenance of ethnoracial and class boundaries around mothering. I had not anticipated this. I had expected to find gendered practices and structured inequalities between men and women in households and in doctor-client relationships in the narratives of the women I interviewed. These were certainly evident. But I also discovered that women produced their mothering cultures largely through engagement with socially homogenous status groups, an engagement that articulated, even enhanced, ethnoracial and class divisions already in place between women. It was in producing these segregating mothering cultures that medicalization acquired meaning in women's lives.

The Jewish respondents forged daily ties to male Jewish physicians and other middle-class Jewish women with whom their medicalized mothering took shape. As I argued in part 1, these daughters of immigrants employed medicalization processes in their move away from immigrants' practices toward modern, American ones. This process of change demanded their participation and membership in new networks of similarly mobile and ambitious Jewish families. The small group of elite African Americans I interviewed also shows a women's medicalized culture and network self-consciously oriented toward class and race cohesion and mobility. In the narratives of this group we find another segregated medicalized culture, one directed around activism and institution building for African Americans. Having less access to medical institutions and practitioners than the Jewish women, these African-American women used their network ties to secure access to the advances of dominant medicine and to economic mobility. Medicalization represented status-group enhancements for both groups of socially mobile mothers and both Jews and African Americans pursued their class concerns through their ethnoracial groups. Yet the nature of the networks' engagements in medicalization differed because of the distinct social pressures and opportunities of their respective social groups.

By contrast, rather than orient their mothering practices to the dominant medical standards, the working-class and working-poor African-American women I interviewed organized mothering in accordance with the norms of reciprocity they developed with others in their social networks who were similarly marginal to medicalization. When these African-American women did connect to whites who were more closely aligned to medical discourse, these were not occasions where established connections could find a place. Rather, they were temporary alliances marked more by differences than coming together across ethnoracial or class divides. These multiple relations rendered medical discourse a site of social exclusion that made visible their "outsider-within" position in relation to dominant norms of mothering.

Network Ties and the Shaping of Modern
Jewish Motherhood

*When I was raising my children, everything was up-to-
date. There was nothing European about any of my
friends either. There was no European way. Everything
was just United States. . . . Because [we] wanted to
assimilate. This was the best.*

                                        Vivian Harris

We saw in chapter 1 that Jewish women distanced themselves from Russian immigrant cultural identity through their medicalized cultures. If
medicalized mothering moved Jewish mothers away from their parents'
identity and practices, it also moved them toward an identity as middle-
class Americans. Like Vivian, the Jewish women idealized receptivity
to medical discourse, associating cultural and social advance with ad-
herence to dominant medical tenets. Although they believed in the
health benefits that their children gained by their use of medicine, they
also linked these practices with their changing social ties and position.
This was not an individual effort; mothers, when doing it, were identifying with and becoming a part of social networks of other middle-class,
socially mobile Jews. Vivian explains that raising her family as American took place within the context of her middle-class Jewish ties:

> I mean, we were just, you know, average. We went to syna-
> gogue. We belonged to a synagogue. And they went to Hebrew
> School and stuff like that. We always mingled with Jewish
> people.

Vivian's creation of a medicalized culture and modern motherhood was
tied to her participation in this network of "Jewish people," a network
which helped to define and allowed her to enact the new American
mother she desired to become.

Jewish as well as African-American women's narratives were
"dense" with markers of ethnoracial belonging and boundary making
(Frankenberg 1993). These women considered themselves, and were
treated as, socially and politically distinct from the white, dominant
mainstream. Sociologist Ruth Frankenberg explains minority women's
heightened capacity to define their ethnoracial distinctiveness compared
to whites, because their "cultures are viewed as separate or different from

normativeness" (1993:229). Most white women, for example, fail to see the culturally or racially distinct dimensions of their ethnoracial location precisely because of its normative power. The women in my study— none of whom is normatively white—provide "rich descriptions" of their mothering practices in ethnoracial terms, precisely because their mothering involved them in reflecting on and creating their position vis-à-vis the white American mainstream. Descriptions of ethnoracial markers are also created collectively to produce the salience of their ethnoracial group, a process explained by Frankenberg: "The production of social and political salience [is] a collective, not an individual, process. [It refers to] the extent to which a group is identified *as* a group, by its own members or by the dominant culture"(1993:215; emphasis in original).

In virtually all the Jewish women's narratives, immersion in socially mobile Jewish networks constituted the primary marker of their Jewishness, more than religious and other cultural practices such as kashrut, facility at speaking Yiddish or Hebrew, or participation in formal religious observance at the synagogue. The women report having a lifelong orientation to forging ties with other Jews, in large part in response to fears of outsiders. Mimi Rubin's comment about her link to other Jews is not unusual: "I never dated a fellow who wasn't Jewish. . . . I was afraid of Italian men" who lived nearby. This was a network tie that had a material basis; most explain that when they worked outside the home, typically before they were married, it was with other Jews, and that their husbands and fathers (and in some cases, mothers) typically also worked for or among other Jews. Furthermore, virtually all the women discuss having lived in, or moved to, or wanting to move to upwardly mobile Jewish neighborhoods (Moore 1981). Rose Kleiner provides an example of the daily culture and material basis of the Jewish community around which she defined her mothering:

> Everybody talked about their children. Everybody walked with their carriage and you walked up to the corner. There was a kosher butcher. And then you walked another block and there were all the stores. There was a store called Gollop's and he carried everything under the sun. There was a butter and egg store and that's what we did.

Creating this environment of ethnoracial and class homogeneity and honoring their economic ties to it was a part of a Jewish woman's obligation, as she decided where to work, whom to marry, how and where to raise her children, where to shop, and which peers and physicians to consult about child health. It was also a response to fears of anti-Semitism and the realities of Jews' exclusion from jobs and neighborhoods (Heinze 1990; Moore 1981). Thus, it was within the "Jewish neighborhood" context that Jewish women cultivated their class aspirations and developed their mothering cultures.

With the proliferation of managed care and centralized medical centers in the late twentieth century, it is hard for us to imagine "the neighborhood doctor." But in the Jewish women's narratives, "the neighborhood doctor" emerges as the quintessential figure of modern medicine. Sylvia Epstein reports that she "kept up with the needles [inoculations] because Dr. Jacobs was close by and I could always walk. I'd wheel [the baby] over to his office, 'cause he was in the neighborhood." She located her doctor through a recommendation her husband received in his "neighborhood business." Mimi associates her trust and reliance on Dr. Copeland to the general "neighborhood's" assessment of his worthiness:

> I was lucky with the doctors I had. They were really good . . .
> 'cause they listened. You know, you could call them on the
> phone. And this Dr. Copeland he came right to the house. I
> mean if he thought a child needed him he was right there.
> Which was good. And the whole neighborhood was just crazy
> about him.

And Judith Kleinman describes the doctor she used during her pregnancy as a member of her "neighborhood":

> He lived on Sixth Street. I lived on Main Street. It was two
> blocks apart. And if you went to his office it was a dollar. And
> if he came to your house it was two dollars. I didn't know
> anybody to go to. He was a doctor that was in the neighborhood and everybody used him and I was using him too. And he
> was a great guy. He really was. He was wonderful. . . . You sit
> and you talk to people. Everybody used Dr. Hoont. So I went to
> Dr. Hoont.

Yet the neighborhood doctor held significance in ways that extended beyond geographic convenience. What these women refer to

as "the neighborhood" actually is the homogenous network of other upwardly mobile middle-class Jews. This network was composed of other
households and families very much like their own; children of immigrants who were geared toward the modern developments and signs of
social progress. It was within these networks that their physicians were
located. With very few exceptions, the physicians that Jewish women
referred to in their narratives were Jewish men.

Indeed, it was a physician's immersion in a common Jewish social
network that provided the foundation for women's faith in him. Unlike other immigrant groups, Jews had many physicians in their personal
networks (Danzi 1997; Watkins and Danzi 1995). Rose Kleiner, for example, explained that she "used the best pediatrician for [my daughter]
Phyllis." I asked her how she knew that he was the best: "Well, in the
first place, he happened to be my mother's cousin." Many women described the feeling of personal intimacy they developed with the physician, largely from the sense that the physician was located in their
social network. Estelle Sein explains that she preferred going to Jewish
doctors:

> Because I could talk [to them]. I don't know. I felt that they
> would understand me better or whatever. I think you could talk
> more openly with a person of your own religion. . . . That doesn't
> mean that Christian doctors aren't good doctors. They probably
> are. But you felt, I felt more at ease with a Jewish doctor.

These relations were sometimes invoked in sexual terms. One recalls
that she liked the physician so much that, "He could have put his shoes
under my bed anytime."

It was through a gendered framework that these Jewish women
forged their ties to these Jewish physicians. As men—neighbors, broth-
ers, friends—pursued medical degrees or other business and professional
opportunities to achieve their own social advance, mothers promoted
their social position by reshaping their households and mothering orientation, transforming them to meet American ideals. Many women
took pride in their ability to be full-time mothers. But others were more
aware that this limited their own opportunities, as Vivian explains:

> It was before the war and not too many married women were
> working. And that fact that I worked after I got married, you

know, everybody got married and quit. . . . And then I became pregnant and quit. Nobody worked while they were pregnant then. That was the thing to do then. That's ridiculous, isn't it? . . . I remember when Esther was little and she got up at six, and I'd stand there in [the] front window holding her and I watched the women going to work and I was so envious. I was so envious.

These women fully understood that pursuing a career in medicine was something that only men could do. Many women explained that having a son become a doctor was the dream of their Jewish parents. Diana Brown offers one example, describing her parents' support of her brother's hope to become a physician and the restrictions that support placed on her own career opportunities:

> [My brother] Sol was the first Jewish scholar to get a mayor's scholarship to the [University of Pennsylvania]. . . . And the rest of us, you know, we went through high school and it was during the Depression. One sister, she was a technician. But by the time I got out of high school, in thirty-three, there really wasn't any money to send me any further. I wanted to be a nurse and of course that was all wiped out. Let me put it this way. The standard of living in my family, even when my parents were doing well, was not like it is today, or nowhere near it, because they didn't know my brother was going to get a scholarship and the only aim in their life was to see that their son would be a doctor.

Diana explains why her parents' desire was so strong:

> Well, I think the European people and Jewish people, even to this day, when their son is a doctor they have accomplished a lot. That means that he wouldn't have to stand on his feet and take the stuff from the customers. They found that it was really the peak, if their son was a doctor. But a doctor, everybody knew a doctor was really something. So that even when they had a little more, everything was for Sol's education.

Jewish men, when possible, signaled their social advance by obtaining this or another professional credential. Jewish women, rather than become doctors themselves, supported this socially mobile group of men by consulting them and honoring their authority. As a "sign of respect," for example, Barbara Schwartz referred to her cousin, a physician, not as Harry but as "Dr. Schwartz." Indeed, the women I interviewed took great pride in connecting their mothering, their household, and their child care to this group of socially mobile men.

These women forged their connections to this group in some cases by the cooking they (or their mothers) did for the visiting physician. Sadie Horowitz reports that she exchanged her mother's strudel for her physician's medical services, a practice that connected the doctor and Sadie to a common ethnic group through the gendered relations of cooking:

> My mother was a very good cook. And [the doctor] would go into [my parents'] store, most of the time he would go into the store and see what she had to offer him before he would go upstairs [to my apartment]. And like he said for the payment for taking care of my daughter's hand "Your mother will make me a box of strudel." And we took it up to him. "Oh," [he said], "paid in full."

The doctor's acceptance of the strudel (a common Jewish food) and Sadie's mention of its importance expresses their ethnoracial status commonality as much as it attests to the quality of her mother's baking. Through cooking, women worked at maintaining and producing their status commonality with these men (DeVault 1991; DiLeonardo 1984).

Selma Cohen's bond to her Jewish physician also emerged in these gendered and ethnoracial terms. She describes the physician she consulted for her pregnancies and deliveries as "a real neighborhood doctor where on a Friday night he'd come in and play cards with the family, with my husband's family; they all lived on the same street." She saved the instruction sheets Dr. Raskin gave her in 1940 and showed them to me. Along with the formulas for bottle-feeding, "pablum," and "pear pineapple Jell-O," Dr. Raskin recommended "chicken liver, lox, and herring," characteristically Jewish foods. Indeed, following Dr. Raskin's prescription is significant in this respect not only because it specifies Selma's gendered obligation to cook but also because it combines ethnoracial and expert cultures.

Reference to physicians as known and trusted figures within their networks points to the importance of the status group in women's constructions of medicalization. Jewish foods, such as strudel, chicken liver, lox, and herring, as well as the personal comfort of talking to a Jewish physician, enabled women to enact their common ethnoracial and class identity through their gendered practices of mothering. The relationship both validated communal ties and expressed their importance. The relationship also connected the women to a network of other mothers much like themselves.

Women's Networks and the Legitimation of Medical Authority

When we had children . . . we'd all talk. The friends
would get together and talk. It was a whole new
life. . . . We just thought it was better. Doctor[s] knew
more than we did.

Mimi Rubin

If medical authority gained its attractiveness because it was transmitted by known and important community figures in the context of familiar ethnoracial and gender traditions and social ambitions, it gained much of its power because it connected mothers to a socially advanced status group of Jewish women who were similarly oriented toward modernization and advancement.

Diana Brown points out her identification with the collectively held standards of her new status group as she levels criticisms against old-fashioned remedies. By participating in the normative practices of her community, Diana identifies herself as an insider to it:

> Once in a while I would give an enema [to my child], once in a while. But then nobody else did. You know you talk to your neighbor, your girlfriends, they have children. They stopped too and it was just a thing of the past. Things became more modern. You just didn't do that.

Diana's contrast between "a thing of the past" and "things became more modern" brings together her sense of a social world that was changing and her placement of herself as participating in these changes. It was not as an isolated individual that her participation in this new world of modernity was structured, but as a part of a collectivity of mothers who were similarly positioned.

Women's mothering was constructed around daily interactions with other women in their community. It was through their participation in these interactions that women cultivated their ties to medicine. Women tell stories of friendships and conversations that virtually always included the sharing of medical information (Watkins and Danzi 1995). Esther Miller shows the physician's advice as a typical feature of women's culture:

> In those days you were a group of women that lived on the street and you were like family. You knew exactly what she was feeding her kid or you were feeding your kid. It was a closeness that . . . women don't have nowadays. . . . We'd get up in the morning and the woman next door that I'm still friendly with, when you open our back door there was one common platform that you went down for the back steps. And so, one morning she would make coffee or tea and one morning I would make coffee. And we would have breakfast together and we would compare notes. Her son was constipated and we would compare notes. [He] was always in terrible pain and the doctor said to give him grapes. And this one had this or the woman down the street didn't use soy milk, her kids were allergic so she used goat's milk. You found out different things that way.

Going to the doctor was a shared social activity, as Sadie Horowitz explains:

> [My friends and I] used to confer . . . if one had a cold or something. Being we used the same doctors and things, a lot of times I'd go with her when she'd take Arlene for a checkup and she'd go with me, you know. We were that close. And we did use the same doctor, Dr. Weidman. I was using him first. And then she automatically, just 'cause I was using him, she liked him.

Sharing the doctor and visiting him together were expressions of "closeness" between these two women; their mutual reliance on him signified the intimacy between them.

Esther points to the priority that her friendship network gave to medical intervention. Her baby son was not eating well and was having difficulty breathing. It was the community of women that finally intervened and enabled Esther to consult a specialist:

> You could hear [my son] breathing three blocks away. . . . He couldn't breathe well and here I was trying to breast-feed him, not knowing that he was very allergic and I was just killing him, you know. . . . When he was so ill that he couldn't breathe this woman across the street said "You have to have a doctor for this baby." So I remember, we called a Dr. Einstein. She had told me that he was a kind doctor and he wouldn't charge too much money and so she said "You have to go." I went to his office. And he said that we had to see a man by the name of Victor Miller, he was an ear, nose, and throat specialist. And he was up in Chestnut Hill. And I remember he wanted twenty-five dollars for the visit. We didn't have twenty-five dollars. Everybody chipped in and I got together twenty-five dollars. This woman told that woman, this woman told this woman, and we got together the twenty-five dollars.

Esther's narrative speaks to the daily presence and validation of medical authority. Physicians appear in their narratives as involved in the routine details of child care and child illness and as part of the wider women's culture around which mothering was organized. The referrals, the collection of money, the monitoring of one another's children in relation to the doctor's orders all served to uphold the importance of physicians' involvement in women's practices.

It is particularly ironic that these networks of women generated the context of women's ties to medicine, because in medical understandings these networks were precisely those that threatened medical authority (Litt 1993). And yet, the narratives show that it was within the context of these ties that medical discourse gained its significance, as it connected women to this upwardly mobile status group. And because it was in networks of women that physicians received their reputations and became familiar, these networks had some control over how physicians were evaluated and employed. The referral system served as an important way that these women collaborated in the consolidation of the power of medical expertise but at the same time provided them with some control over medical intervention (Freidson 1970).

Insiders, Outsiders, and Medicalized Mothering

To understand how status cultures function we must examine how distinctions between groups function both "to exclude others and to constitute collective identity within groups" (Hall 1992:262). Jewish mothers relied upon and trusted medical authority within the context of their Jewish middle-class group: they consulted Jewish physicians and participated in Jewish networks. In this section I examine further how Jewish mothers drew and negotiated boundaries between insiders in and outsiders to this status group. In forging these ties to their status group the Jewish women produced a segregating culture of medicalized motherhood.

We can see this process of differentiation in women's discussions of the relationships they developed with the domestic workers they employed. Like medicalization, employing a housekeeper signaled for many of these women their economic and social success (Rollins 1985). Of the eighteen women, six discussed employing domestic workers when their children were small. Their relationships with these employees were functional and highly demarcated from the rest of the Jewish women's social ties. Domestics did the cooking and, as Barbara explains, the "menial work," while their employers cared for children. Judith describes the status improvement that enabled her to hire a domestic worker:

> After my husband got a half-way decent [job], a very prestigious
> job, [I hired a housekeeper]. He became a milk man and he was
> considered top priority for credit. Thirty-five dollars a week.
> And everybody's making twenty dollars a week.

When I asked Judith whether she spoke to her housekeeper about the children, she replied:

> They never used to do that. Today, they're a little bit more
> sociable than they were at that time. I spoke to her [but] I
> didn't sit down and socialize with her. I would say, "Nellie,
> you're going to do this."

Judith was not alone in her resistance to sharing child care knowledge with hired domestics. When I asked these women whether they discussed child health or child care with the women they employed they stated emphatically that they did not. In this most intimate of environments, these women, working together in the household, did not exchange information.

Relations between domestics and their employers were often relations of distance, ones that reflected ethnoracial and class tensions. To illustrate this distance, Judith describes her mother-in-law's experience with the "colored women" who were looking for domestic work:

> Years ago they used to have day workers. They congregated on the corner of Seventh and Porter Street with the colored men. And they knew that when somebody, especially on a Friday, if somebody wanted somebody's house scrubbed the women would come there and ask a girl to go. And they charged five dollars a day which was a lot of money. So my mother-in-law used to look them over, this one's too fat, this one's too short, this one's not strong enough. And she'd feel their muscles even. Anyway she picked [one woman] out. She says "Would you like [a] day's work? You want a day's work, come on with me." So she comes, she takes her home. [She asks,] "You ate breakfast? No. You want some breakfast?" She scrambled some eggs and coffee and toast and the poor woman got done eating and she threw a quarter on the table and she said "Here's a tip. I always wanted a white woman to wait on me." And walked out of the house!

I asked Judith how her mother-in-law responded:

> She couldn't hardly speak English. I mean she was helpless. Colored women used to stand on the corner and laugh at these people. Make fun of them. It was a ghetto. A Jewish ghetto.

Judith emphasizes the workers' contempt for her mother and other Jews of the "Jewish ghetto" in part as a marker of the difference and conflict between these groups of women. The institution of paid domestic work provided one of the few contexts in which Jewish and African-American women had frequent contact, but in practice this contact reinforced the ethnoracial and class divisions between them (Clark-Lewis 1994; Dill 1994; Palmer 1989; Rollins 1985).

Medicalization may seem an unlikely place to find the production of these social divisions among women. According to dominant medical rationales, scientific knowledge and applications promised to standardize motherhood practices. With its (purportedly) universal and objective language of science, dominant medicine was alleged to erode divisions between ethnoracial groups, forging women's common participation in a new culture of health. Yet as these Jewish women participated in medical discourse they constructed a segregated network of mothers and treated medical discourse not as a technical system but a site of class, gender, and ethnoracial exclusivity. Following their lead, we can view medical discourse as a collectively constructed cultural resource that signified and granted membership in the socially desirable group.

As sociologists of culture argue, some cultural resources cultivate differences, functioning not with open boundaries but with guarded ones; those boundaries that are most highly restricted uphold the unequal distribution of social resources (Gans 1992; Lamont and Fournier 1992). Medical discourse, despite the openness claimed for it by the ideology of science, offers an example of a guarded boundary that secured its meaning as a site of social division. Feeling part of a new, upwardly mobile group helped women articulate their differences from outsiders.

Selma offers another example of how this distancing operated to separate mothers into different categories. We have heard her justify consulting Dr. Raskin by explaining that "Everybody went to Dr. Raskin"; here she explains why she didn't discuss her child with her next door neighbor:

> And this one neighbor who lived next door to me was not like I was. I mean, she didn't believe. She took her children to a doctor occasionally when they were sick. She did the rudimentary things. She took them to a health clinic for injections and things, where I went to a private doctor. She didn't do the reading that I did. She didn't teach her children like I did.

Part of Selma's health-related work involved distinguishing which mothers were possible to confide in. Like other women, Selma drew boundaries between insiders and outsiders constantly as she created distinctions between herself and others. When her daughter was born, Selma decided to consult a pediatrician rather than continue to use the general practitioner. Selma explained her decision by referring both to her new social mobility and to her absorption in the values held by her new community:

> Why? I guess because, eh, well, maybe by the time my daughter was born I was a little, my husband was making a little, doing a little better. I had known him [Dr. Raskin] from friends of mine who had babies and they all used him and he was, oh, his name was very well known in the South Philadelphia area where I went. Everybody went to Dr. Raskin.

Sarah Rosenfeld also identifies her new reliance on a private doctor as a signifier of her changing status group membership. In this narrative, she compares her use of a "clinic" in her former neighborhood with using her "own doctor" in the new one. Sarah emphasizes her family's improving financial picture, and highlights how her move to a more economically prosperous neighborhood reflected her entrance into a more privileged group of mothers:

> All these poor people, poor people in need that didn't have, you know, would go to a clinic. With my third child, my mother was gone, and we lived in Logan and it was a whole different scene. It was a whole different scene . . . because everybody had their own doctor. . . . We all used the same doctor and I was the first one to use this doctor because he was recommended by this Dr. Greenspan. . . . God, oh my God, yeah. He was just like one of us, yeah.

Sarah's newly achieved ability to pay for a private physician signaled more than her improving financial position. It marked her increasing social distance from the "poor people" with whom she had previously associated and identified, and it allowed her to perceive herself as being personally affiliated with and socially similar to the physician she consulted: "He was just like one of us." Using the medicalized practices of these social networks of mothers and physicians signified Sarah's improving social position.

Barbara discusses "reaching out" to a "better world" which included physicians, living in a Jewish neighborhood, and identifying with a "better class" of Jews:

> Your eyes are open. You know. You hear. When I started to work steady in the hospital the other girls came from Wynfield,

from West Philadelphia. That was a whole new world to me. I never lived in Wynfield but it was known as the better class Jew lived there. And the girls came in fashionable stuff you know, and they looked well and I knew there was things that I wasn't a part of. I guess subconsciously that was my reaction, I don't know. . . . Nobody handed me anything. I can tell you that. . . . You plugged away the best you could. And some reached it. Some didn't and that's it.

We can see this association between social position and mothering practices vividly in Estelle's narrative below. She was the one Jewish mother who remained distant from modern medical discourse, who remained largely tied to immigrant parents and practices. Her narrative provides a view of middle-class Jewish social life from the outside. She describes it with a mixture of regret and relief:

Some of [my friends were breast-feeding]. Some. Some were a little better off and they knew a little more. But I never even knew what a bottle was. . . . There were people there who made a living, who made more money, who could afford different things. . . . Afterwards, after [my children] grew up and I knew what was going on, [I thought] "Jeez, what did I do? How did I raise my kids?" . . . Breast-feeding them, giving them food from the table. I'm very glad, being in the circumstances that we were, I was very glad that I didn't know any better. If I would know better, if I knew that people didn't have to cook and people didn't have to clean, they had girls come in and clean, they had—they bought all kinds of fancy goods or whatever, I would have been very unhappy. . . . [And] I was so busy taking care of the home, taking care of my mother, that who knew what was doing in other places? I didn't know what a department store was.

While Barbara, Selma, and Sarah position themselves within the new medicalized culture of advanced Jewish families, Estelle places herself outside the momentum of new social and technological developments in large part by emphasizing her social and personal isolation, her existence on the margins of the middle-class group of women who "were a little better off and . . . knew a little more." Here she draws an explicit connection between social class position and domestic practice.

Seeing herself outside the social group where these modern practices took place, Estelle also places herself outside the catch of medical techniques. In her view from the margin, Estelle understands that medicalization functioned as a shared, common pursuit among like-minded and similarly situated individuals, and that it involved her own exclusion.

A final dimension of this boundary construction is in the boundaries Jewish mothers drew between Jews and Gentiles. This was a distinction that formulated their identity as mothers, and thus was fundamental in how they constructed their medicalized culture of mothering. It was not until the postwar years that Jews became defined as "whites," according to Brodkin (1998). It was in a liminal position—as both insiders and outsiders—that these women marked the borders of their mothering cultures. While these women spoke of themselves and other Jews as having finally achieved the status of insiders in the United States in relation to their immigrant backgrounds, they had one eye looking back toward Europe's atrocities. It was not only in relation to past anti-Semitism that these Jewish women constructed their new identities. They were raising their children during the time when Adolf Hitler achieved power in Germany and nearly killed all of Europe's Jews. Here we find women describing danger in their present context, a danger these women concealed when discussing their own advance from Russian persecution but one that pervaded the notions of mothering they idealized.

Diane Weinberg, who lived above the family's dry-cleaning business in North Philadelphia, spoke of protecting her son from her non-Jewish neighbors because of this fear:

> When [my son] was all of two years, I bought boxing gloves. . . .
> I never left him on his own. I always took him outside. 'Cause I
> want you to know we were surrounded by Nazis and Irish,
> mostly German. The grocer at two doors away had Hitler on
> [the radio].

It was in this context of fear that she wanted to isolate her son from non-Jews, as she explains:

> I sent him to Hebrew school when he was five years old because
> I didn't want him around these kids. [My son's friend] was
> Catholic and Irish and Larry wanted to go to the [public] school

because he was so crazy about him. I say, "No. You're not going there. We don't belong there." So . . . I put him [in Hebrew School] to get away. He never was around [the neighborhood]. In fact, June the first to Labor Day I would go to Atlantic City.

Diane's desire to live among other Jews was shared among the Jewish women I interviewed. Mimi reveals a solution that many mothers chose; she moved to a neighborhood where "everybody knew everybody," where, in effect, the vast majority of her neighbors were Jewish women like herself. Her house hunting involved a search for markers of Gentileness and Jewishness, markings she thought could provide information about safety for her children:

At Fifty-eighth and Warrington was a big synagogue. And my kids were active there and they always say it was the best place to grow up. When I went to look for my house, I went during Christmas week because you could tell how many goyim lived in the neighborhood and it was just one wreath and they were Greeks and they were the nicest people. That was the best neighborhood to grow up in 'cause everybody knew everybody. Everybody, I mean, they were so friendly, so nice. And [my kids] naturally grew up with Jewish children.

The commonality mothers worked to create demanded the exclusion of others and gave rise to a situation of mothering that took place principally among Jewish middle-class social groups. This particularism, rooted in the constant creation of boundaries between types of mothers, is ironic, finally, because it cuts against the universalized discourse that these mothers invoke to explain their reliance on medicine—their "modernity," their "Americanness," and their "ethicality." Although mothers use these signifiers of universalized discourse in their explanations of what medicalization meant, they do not construct their medicalized practices as translatable across ethnoracial or class lines; it appears as if such movement robbed them of their value.

Barbara describes her movement from an ethnically mixed to a Jewish neighborhood as a movement toward safe and trustworthy knowledge about child care:

The worst thing was that I [had previously] moved away from my family. . . . All my married sisters lived in a radius of one

block, and don't forget we lived with my mother. And here I
am going into this wilderness with no Jews because . . . where
we had our [pharmacy] business was Italian, Irish, and some
black. Not knowing anything, but somehow or other the Lord
looks and then I never had it so good, let me just tell you. We
worked our butts off. . . . Then we moved after that. . . . I
decided that uh, it was time to bring them into a, what I
thought, to meet some Jewish friends.

Defining the absence of Jews as a "wilderness," Barbara sets herself
off from these other outsiders with whom she did not want to be identified yet with whom she shared her neighborhood and on whom her
family's business depended. Feeling alone, threatened, and fearful in this
terrain of an ethnoracially mixed neighborhood, feeling no comfort from
the insights of these neighbors, she appears to have lost her capacity to
"know anything;" instead she relied on the Lord. It was only when she
was securely situated with Jewish friends that she felt able to depend
on her community for child health and mothering support. The community of Jews Barbara eventually joined allowed her to feel that her
children—and her mothering behavior—were less vulnerable. Her move
to a Jewish middle-class suburb emerges in this context as the reward
for sacrifice and hard work.

As a further illustration, consider Sylvia's comment that she did
not talk to her Catholic neighbors about her children's health:

I think I was the only Jewish family on that street. I lived on
Rosalie Street. . . . It's Catholic. And, uh, I really never did, I
never remember talking about the children, no. You know I
never did, I don't know why. Not that I resented them in any
way but I just didn't.

I asked Sylvia what that had to do with being Jewish and them being
Catholic:

I, I don't know. Now that you brought it up, I don't know. . . .
Pauline next door had Billy, and uh, I never spoke to her about
what doctor or anything she went to. I never did. Uh, whether
it had something to do because maybe I thought they didn't
know as much.

What Diane, Barbara, and Sylvia reveal is that securing health for children, being a good mother, involved joining and helping to create status groups of similarly situated people—maternal work deeply steeped in learning how to discern insiders from outsiders. Medical discourse here emerges not as a universal discourse that was shared across ethno-racial groups, but as a cultural practice that gained its authority and meaning as it marked women's membership in an exclusive, advancing, and protective social network. Mothers engaged in reflexive distancing between themselves and others as they recreated themselves as dependent on medical authority.

Chapter 5

"We Tried to Work with Our People"

African-American Upper-Middle-Class Networks and the Making of Medicalized Motherhood

Like the Jewish women I interviewed, the upper-middle-class African-American mothers used physicians who were personally known to them or their families and forged network ties that were self-consciously socially segregating. Also like the Jewish women, they pursued class interests through their association with these networks and spoke of them as the site where their family's social advance and good health were fostered. Yet these mothers present different kinds of network relations than the Jewish women; they focus not as much on the everyday, informal relations of life in a socially homogenous neighborhood and more on establishing formal network ties to others in their class and ethno-racial group who were dispersed through the city, ties which secured access to middle-class institutions for their children. Responding to a racially divided city and medical establishment, these women used their racial and class-based networks as levers for breaking down racial barriers.

Attempting to eliminate the racism in medicine and gaining access to medical advance was a struggle that was waged in and through these networks. We do not hear these women desire a return to folk remedies but rather express a focused conviction that access to dominant medical technologies and institutions (as both patients and practitioners) was essential to African-American survival. In fact, within the wider African-American community, gaining access to medical care was a battle forged along the same front as the civil rights struggle generally. This context of exclusion and activism defined the relation the upper-middle-class African-American women developed to medical discourse.

We turn first to consider how African Americans fought to change the medical system, and then to narratives of women's network ties and relations to medical discourse. A focused case study of two women, Sue Thompson and Marion Marks, provides insight into the link between medicalization and upper-middle-class African-American women's networks, which is different from the link for Jewish women, and, as we see in chapter 6, different from the one for poor and working-class African-American women.

Negro Health Week and Health Activism

Since early in the twentieth century, African-American club and church women, the NAACP, the Urban League, and major African-American leaders of the time such as Booker T. Washington, Roscoe C. Brown, and W.E.B. DuBois, linked racial segregation with the damaged health of African Americans (Beardsley 1987; Carson 1994; McBride 1989; Smith 1995). In 1915 Washington spelled out this connection: "Without health . . . it will be impossible for us to have permanent success in business, in property getting, [and] in acquiring education. . . . Without health and long life all else fails. We must reduce our high death-rate, dethrone disease and enthrone health and long life" (quoted in Smith 1995:38). And since the late nineteenth century, African Americans have fought for federal support for improvement in medical services and have relied largely on the daily, and often invisible, work of African-American women to bring the advances of public health to communities (Smith 1995). It is worth taking a brief detour to explain the history of the black health movement, for it anticipated many of the needs and responses developed among the upper middle class in Philadelphia.

In 1915, Booker T. Washington, founder of the Tuskegee Institute, began the health education campaign known as National Negro Health Week. Run out of the education wing of the Tuskegee Institute, the campaign developed community-level public health activities to promote African Americans' health through such activities as education on hygiene, sanitation, and baby care, and developed new services such as playgrounds, visiting nurses, free clinics, and trash removal. The movement, according to medical historian Susan L. Smith (1995), built on black women's club work of community reform begun in the late nineteenth century. While women continued to perform the community level outreach, men took the campaign to the national level, bringing the health problems of both southern and northern African Americans to the attention of the federal government.

In 1932 the federal government responded to these campaigns, establishing the United States Public Health Service's Office of Negro Health Work. This office coordinated the National Negro Health Week campaigns across the country and served as a clearinghouse for health research and activism on behalf of African Americans. Smith argues that this new office, established among the New Deal programs from which African Americans were generally excluded, marked a turning point in the history of American public health; it was the first time since the post–Civil War era that the United States government institutionalized African-American health concerns as a feature of the federal system. Yet, according to Smith, community health work continued to rest on the daily work of women, without whom most African-American communities would not have received the benefits of public health services or education.

Philadelphia had its own health movement that developed along a track parallel to that of the national movement (Alston 1987; McBride 1989) and it was within this context that the women I interviewed forged their ties to medicine. In the years between the World Wars, according to medical historian David McBride, "two worlds" of medicine existed in Philadelphia, "one black and one white" (1989:xvii). The city's medical system was almost entirely segregated. As late as World War II it was still the case that twelve of the city's hospitals would admit black patients only in "colored wards." Other discriminatory practices included separate attendance hours with long waiting periods, verbal abuse by white hospital staff, lack of maternal and child health facilities, and a shortage of chronic care and convalescence facilities. These factors, combined with poverty and poor housing, produced higher than average morbidity and mortality rates among African

Americans. Infant and maternal mortality rates were higher among blacks than whites in the United States generally, and in the period between 1933 and 1935 the rate per 1,000 live births in Pennsylvania was 84.3 for African Americans and 51.4 for whites (McBride 1989).

In 1937 Dr. Virginia Alexander, one of ninety African-American women physicians in the nation (Alexander-Minter 1986), produced a report strongly critical of the appalling conditions African Americans faced in Philadelphia's medical care system. The report focused on the lack of hospital facilities for African Americans in North Philadelphia, home to the third-largest concentration of African Americans in the nation. North Philadelphia's medical services compared badly to those of South and West Philadelphia where physicians could admit patients to Douglass and Mercy Hospitals, the city's two black hospitals. In North Philadelphia, Alexander reported, hospitals and clinics discriminated against African-American patients and professionals in ways even more horrendous than in other parts of the city. Some had separate clinic hours for African Americans, some had "Negro Wards," some refused to admit black women's maternity cases and often did not follow up on discharged patients. Others sent inexperienced medical students to administer childbirth in poor black women's homes. African-American medical practitioners were not permitted into the major teaching hospitals and medical centers in the city, and hence often could not follow their patients when they were admitted to the hospital. Being largely in private practice, these physicians were economically vulnerable and professionally isolated.

Dr. Alexander's report was pivotal in calling attention to the severe health crisis African Americans faced, and was instrumental in the wave of health reform initiated by black professionals in Philadelphia following World War II. The late 1940s witnessed a "new militancy" among African Americans "for the right to equal employment, training, and medical treatment in the nation's health institutions [which] was fast becoming a central current in a stream of local and national black protest" (McBride 1989:149).

In the years before reform, the time period relevant here, African Americans in the city sustained their own hospitals, clinics, and networks of assistance. Within this context of racial segregation and isolation, professionals and activists developed extensive ties that were oriented to improving the welfare of the city's black population. The result, according to McBride, was the development of a separate layer of medical associations and health facilities that were generated and sustained by the city's African-American leadership. Dr. Virginia Alexander (1900–1949) was one of the prominent members of this network. She was born to a poor family in Philadelphia, one of four children. Her eldest brother, Raymond Pace Alexander, was to become a major African-American lawyer and judge in the city. Despite having faced extreme racial discrimination through her training and practice, by 1933 she was on staff at the Hospital of the Women's Medical College of Pennsylvania (her alma mater) and Douglass Hospital (one of the city's two black hospitals), and on the outpatient staff at Pennsylvania Hospital. In 1928 she opened the Aspiranto Health Home, a hospital and health center in a row house she converted in North Philadelphia. There patients came for deliveries, for two-weeks-postnatal care, and for instruction in raising babies. Others could get general medical care, such as tonsillectomies. She opened the health center to serve the poor African Americans in North Philadelphia, although middle-class women used the facility as well. Alexander described her practice in a letter she wrote to her prospective partner, Dr. Helen Dickens, in 1935:

> My practice is larger, but by no means lucrative. I have accumulated nothing in the way of the world's goods; but I think I have established a fairly sound practice. I am busy sixteen hours a day. . . . My whole health plan savors of a type of socialized practice of medicine, the evolution of which would develop as we caught the vision of community service. (quoted in Alexander-Minter 1986:2–3)

I was fortunate in my interviewing to meet Dr. Dickens, who practiced with Dr. Alexander in the Aspiranto Health Home. Dickens was born in Dayton, Ohio. Her mother was the daughter of farmers and her father, until he was eight years old, was a slave in Kentucky. After facing her own racial discrimination in applications to medical school she was finally admitted to the University of Illinois College of Medicine. After graduation, she spent two years in obstetric training and general practice at Provident Hospital in Chicago, from 1934 to 1935 and then from 1942 to 1943. She was a resident in obstetrics and gynecology at

Harlem Hospital in New York from 1943 to 1946. She then moved to Philadelphia, to be Dr. Alexander's partner at the Aspiranto Health Home. Alexander left the practice the following year to pursue a degree in public health. Dickens stayed at the home for seven years.

Drs. Alexander and Dickens's experience in this work gave them first-hand knowledge of how women's and children's health was jeopardized by the lack of medical care that went along with poverty and an uninviting medical system (Dannert 1966). Dickens explained that many women rarely used the system:

> They used doctors if they had a cold, or the flu, or they hurt themselves, had an injury. But they didn't use 'em for prevention, I guess I'll put it that way. They used them for illness, for need. And they didn't come necessarily when they just got pregnant. They might be three, four, five months pregnant when they came for care.

In Dr. Dickens's descriptions, we find a medical system that was inconvenient and uncomfortable, even indifferent to the health needs of African Americans. Dickens was clear that for poor women and their children, medical care in Philadelphia was not very appealing. Many "dreaded" the Philadelphia General Hospital clinics, where most African Americans in the city received their health care, as she explains:

> They didn't like PGH. They didn't like to go. Probably because of the way they were handled. Not on a personal basis so much as, you know. While it might not have been segregated, they may have been a little negative to them.

Opening the Aspiranto Health Home was a way to get women the medical care they needed. Dr. Dickens explains:

> Because women wouldn't go or didn't go to the hospital . . . when they were pregnant or had other problems, if they didn't have to go. And, um, we were delivering babies at home. . . . This was a step before the hospital. They would come to [Dr. Alexander]. And if they needed to have care, she would give it to them there 'cause they would deliver at home otherwise. With or without adequate care.

She continued by explaining some of the conditions their patients lived in:

> I can remember one night [during a house call for a delivery]. They didn't have any electricity or any other kind of light. So we pushed the patient to the window so we could use the streetlight to deliver the baby. So that [as a doctor] you really were there on your own. So that was, some of the things the women would come to [Dr. Alexander with]. I guess because they knew that she would take care of them, and she would usually take care of women [whether they] had any money or not.

Dr. Dickens describes a problem that had been identified by the African-American leadership: white medical interns were being dispatched, without supervision, to deliver the babies of indigent African-American women:

> One night when I was in the office . . . a couple of students from Temple [University] came and asked me, they were seeing something [in a delivery nearby]. They didn't know what they were looking at, and would I come over. And I said, "Well, where is your instructor?" They said, "Well, he is tied up somewhere else and he can't just come now." Well I said, "I'm working in my office. I can't just come now either." So I went on working, and pretty soon they came back and said would I please come. So I said, "Okay, I will come." So I went back there, one of those row houses, and I took a look at what they had. And it was a breach. It was a male child. And the scrotum was presenting swollen. They didn't know what it was. They didn't know what they had. And these women [friends and relatives] were standing at the door, "Oh, mugga, mugga, mugga" you know, like they don't know what they're doing, they were worried about the doctors. So I told 'em to just leave the door[way] and shut the door. So I put them out.

Dr. Dickens then worked with the patient, delivered the infant, and explained to the interns what they were looking at. Dickens told me that she wasn't angry about the case, but that "they should have had a backup for these people [instructors] who were busy."

Drs. Dickens and Alexander were part of the citywide network of African-American professionals engaged in producing a safety net for the poor. Along with others, these women created their own solutions to the systematic racism and segregation of the city's medical and social system. Like others in the African-American medical community, they tackled poverty and racism as they confronted the daily health conditions their low-income patients presented. At the same time, they were involved in networks of upper-middle-class African Americans who were oriented toward securing access to the dominant health care system and health stability for their own children.

Mothers' Networks and the Promise of Medicalization: Sue Thompson

I imagine in the eyes of many people, particularly Caucasian American[s], I was quote nontypical. Well, that's not true. I was one of many. Millions. There are thousands of us. . . . I don't think [whites] thought we existed. Whereas, we did exist. Just yesterday, I stopped by my cousin's and had the sad task of reading to him the obituary of one of his best friends, who had just died. He was his dear friend, who graduated from Harvard in 1926. And his father was a doctor before him. He was one of the founders of the United Negro College Fund. And his wife's sister is married to a man who was the president of Tuskegee. . . . It just kills my brain for people to think that we have just been like Topsy and we just growed up all of a sudden.

Sue Thompson

Sue Thompson's insistence on having the history of the African-American professional middle class made visible emerges in part out of her anger about the stereotyping of all African Americans as poor and uneducated. Indeed, as we see in her reflections of growing up in one of these upwardly mobile families, much effort was expended to distinguish her family from others with less education and fewer resources and to tie them to professionals with similar aspirations and mobility.

We met Sue Thompson's parents in chapter 3, which discussed their migration North and their movement into the upper middle class. The Thompsons were in what historian Charles Banner-Haley (1993) calls the new African-American middle class. This middle-class group survived the Great Depression in a much stronger position than did the poor and working class. Their financial resources declined, but their jobs most often maintained them at a good standard of living. They worked in medicine, law, funeral homes, and churches, where employment remained relatively secure during the Depression. Barbershop and beauty parlor owners also managed relatively well, as their stores were social centers. Simultaneously, the middle class pictured itself as providing a model of hard work and thrift, to which working-class and poor individuals could aspire.

Sue understood that her parents lived within a tightly knit group of members of the upper middle class. Much like the Jewish women, she represents the network as self-consciously oriented toward producing and maintaining class privileges through racially homogenous ties. Yet it was not through informal neighborhood relations but through formal connections that this network aided the careers of African-American professionals, as Sue explains:

> All the North Philadelphia people knew each other and all the West Philadelphia people knew each other and the Germantown people knew [each other]. One of the things, and this is the way that I think we got close to Dr. Dickens, [was] in those days, we would have teas. We had teas from house to house.

One of the houses, she remarks, "actually had a music room." She continues:

> [The house] had a floor-to-ceiling library on one wall. And then the concert grand [piano] and so people used [this] house for the teas. On Sunday afternoons, so what they would do, new professionals coming to town, new professionals would be introduced at a tea. Someone would come in and they would say, "This is the new doctor." I can remember very well that my mother and father did that for Henry Louis and they also did it for Dr. Dickens. And Lloyd, a lawyer. Uh, singers would be introduced there. Doris Manor, who had gone on to be a concert pianist and teacher at Oberlin.

According to Banner-Haley, as the black middle class in Philadelphia positioned itself to improve the condition of the working- and lower-class masses, it was also in the contradictory position of self-consciously struggling to distance itself from them. This put the middle class in a dilemma, caught between "maintaining a class consciousness which was not always in touch with the lower class masses and asserting a racial consciousness which might alienate them from the dominant white society" (1993:62). This pattern is true, to some extent, of Sue's parents, whose social network reflected their isolation from dominant white society and their lack of sustained contact with or reliance on African Americans of other social classes. Looking inward to African Americans of their own social class for community resources was possibly inevitable in a context defined by racism.

It was clearly in the context of racism that Sue understood her parents' reliance on the tightly knit network of African-American professionals. She states that the dominant medical system cared little about the survival of African Americans:

> It's always so interesting historically in America. . . . I mean that they took time to put the Indians on a reservation and put them in a special place, but they really didn't expect slaves to survive so they didn't have to worry about getting them any place 'cause they [thought] in a couple of years they're going to die out, they can't make it, you know. So we don't have to worry about them. I mean, who can say that that's really their thinking but that's the way it comes off.

It was to African-American physicians that Sue's family turned when they wanted medical help. "We didn't have much choice," she reports, "I mean, we weren't as welcome [by white physicians]." Sue explains that part of the discrimination resulted in few African-American specialists:

> The important piece that you need there is that blacks themselves had not the wherewithal to specialize as early. Because it was costly. Some of them had just about gotten their medical education and they would go, then, to school, while they were working. You see. So the specialists became specialists later.

Their network of African-American physicians provided Sue's family with access to the principal specialists in the city. To illustrate how white racism could be overcome through these network ties, Sue describes a childhood incident of racism by white opticians to whom she had been referred by Dr. Fay, an African-American ophthalmologist:

> They were opticians. The guy at the front door, there was the opticians all sat in a row at these stools and you came in and he assigned you or waited for somebody to be ready. And the guy at the door told me that "We're not hiring today and we don't need any help." And I was a teenager, and I said, "What did you say?" And he said, "We're not hiring anybody today. We don't need any help." I said, "Sir, Dr. Fay sent me here to get my glasses."

In describing the barrier she encountered to this medical service and how she overcame it, Sue reports the security provided by her social-network ties, security that was contingent on the social-class and ethnoracial connection forged between her parents and the network of professionals with whom they identified. This, then, is a complicated story about racism in the white medical establishment, where Sue's economic position did not in itself guarantee her access to the dominant medical institutions. It was in having access to and using the resources of her African-American network that she was able to secure the medical services she needed.

Sue gave another example of how her family's social network functioned as a resource for obtaining access to the desired medical care. She told a story about her brother's medical needs and the intervention of Dr. Alexander, who worked to overcome the obstacles her brother faced in receiving specialty care:

> My brother was a perfect case in point. He had so much happen to him, but she never stopped. Oh, [Dr. Alexander] would go [with him] to any specialist needed. He was hit by a car, 'cause he was constantly in the street in our little neighborhood. And he fell out of the second-story window at our business and fractured his skull. And, of course, all of these required specialists. And she saw to it. She went [to the hospital with him]. And my brother was one of the first [black] children to be admitted to Children's Hospital. . . . Dr. Alexander was known for not accepting, I mean, she didn't accept no for an answer. She was fair. And when I say fair, skin. So, they [other doctors]

may have thought she wasn't black, you know. But she fought
for her patients.

Dr. Alexander's work of monitoring her patients in hospitals was featured in an article titled "Can a Colored Woman Be a Physician?" in
the magazine *The Crisis* as helping to combat the discriminatory care
African-American patients would otherwise receive:

> [She spends] an endless amount of time following her patients
> to hospitals, checking on her diagnosis both medical and
> surgical, standing by her patients when operated upon and
> visiting them afterwards. . . . This service probably more than
> anything else has had the effect of staving or definitely dulling
> the edge of increased practices of segregation and discrimina-
> tion in most if not all of the hospitals of Philadelphia.
> (1933:33)

The Jewish women did not talk about their network ties as facili-
tating their access to an anti-Semitic medical system, although given
their general perception that they belonged with other Jews, it seems
fair to say that the immersion in Jewish networks served as a similar
kind of protection.

Mothers' Networks and the Promise of Medicalization: Marion Marks

*Well, it's just like the change of the time. As you see
now, everything is different in the world. Not what it
was when I came along. And it's an adjustment that you
yourself had to make. Not only were you supposed to,
that's what you had to do. You need a doctor. You
needed a doctor.*

                                        Marion Marks

Marion Marks was born in South Carolina in 1909 to an African-
American family that was, in her words, "pretty well situated." Marion,
her parents, and siblings (eventually she had seven) moved to Philadelphia while she was an infant. Her father worked in insurance and
owned timberland down South, and even though he died suddenly and
quite young, Marion's mother was provided for financially and "never

had to work a day in her life." Marion married a schoolteacher who became a principal and they had two children in the early 1930s. She never sought employment, claiming that "I set aside my ability to do what I wanted to do. But I stuck home with my children."

Marion organized her children's feeding according to the new medical recommendations: she fed her baby a bottle every four hours. She describes her feeding practices as dependent on medical intervention and advice but appears not to have been passive in relation to this intervention. This negotiation depended on the dialogue she developed with Dr. Dickens, her children's primary physician:

> Well, the doctors tell you when you come in that you should feed them such and such a time. You know. I never gave my children that night [2:00 A.M.] feeding. I wasn't going to do that. After I washed 'em, they had their bath and they were all settled, I would give them my last feeding and that was it. When they went to bed at night, they were in bed. I asked the doctor "Is it absolutely necessary [to wake them up]" and Dr. Dickens said to me, "Well, that was marvelous [if you skip the feeding]." She said, "If you do it you should teach [the] rest of them to do that." And I would never wake up a baby to feed them because to me it's silly to wake up a baby to feed it when the baby was all right. I just couldn't see it. I needed my rest too.

Clearly, Marion wanted Dr. Dickens's permission and felt proud when she complemented her for her initiative. Yet she also expresses a negotiating power, which comes through in the way she describes the incident. She quotes Dr. Dickens's speech directly and switches from the past tense to the present, taking us with her into the moment of negotiation. "Dr. Dickens said to me, 'Well, that was marvelous, you should teach [the] rest of them.'" Marion's use of direct address stresses Dr. Dickens's authority. At the same time, Marion communicates her own confidence in relation to medical standards—after all, she not only needed her rest but thought it was silly to wake a sleeping baby. Marion was able, with permission, to adapt medical regimens to her own needs in dealing with the medical authorities she so revered.

How did Marion's view of herself as participating in her network's collective social mobility affect her relationship to medical expertise?

Marion attributed meaning to medicine as she drew boundaries around her own social position. Her mother's knowledge, she explains, developed from necessity:

> My mother was born in the South, she was in South Carolina. And, you know, a lot of [time] down there sometimes you didn't always able to get to the doctor. They had midwives. They had a lot of herbs you know that they would use.

I asked her why she did not use her mother's remedies.

> Well, it's just like the change of the time. As you see now, everything is different in the world. Not what it was when I came along. And it's an adjustment that you yourself had to make. Not only were you supposed to, that's what you had to do. You need a doctor. You needed a doctor.

In this passage, Marion does more than distinguish between expert and experiential knowledge systems. She also constructs this distinction to mark a boundary around herself and her social networks—a boundary she sees as evidence of her active participation in the "change of the time." Marion saw herself as moving toward the dominant standards of good mothering. Science held a strong attraction for her, an attraction that was as much a moral pull as a technical one. In turn, she used these practices to create herself as a modern mother; adopting medical standards constituted the practice and sign of her advancing social-class position.

Yet to understand the development of Marion's medicalization it is necessary to discuss how she connects her social status to her association with other upper-middle-class families. Marion defined herself as one of a small group of "first Philadelphians," or "old Philadelphia families," African-American (or, in her term, Negro) professionals (funeral directors, dentists, physicians, nurses, teachers, and business owners), all of whom were tied together across diverse professions, different residential neighborhoods, and varied personal friendship networks by their position as members in a common, and well-developed, social network. In the context of Marion's social ties, we see a conception of motherhood that embraces and depends on networks of similarly situated families, all of which, working together, are oriented toward the social mobility of their children. Her family was part of the tea group that Sue discusses. And as a child she grew up attending the fund-raising fairs sponsored by the African-American Mercy Hospital, as she describes:

> As a little girl I was in ballet and dance school and what not. We used to go, they'd have fairs at the Mercy Hospital out on the grounds. People would come from everywhere to these fairs. And as a dancing group, we would go out, do [a] little dancing and acting like fools, see [laughs].

As a mother herself, Marion worked hard to secure these network affiliations for her children. She devoted much of her mothering to building and consolidating ties within these networks, tying her commitment to mothering to her involvement in them:

> You have to sometimes sacrifice your status in life a little bit if you're going to have children. And if you're not willing to do that then the best thing to do, don't have the children. . . . I followed my children all the way through school. Before they went to school we formed a club of just friends. And we brought our children together so they would know each other. . . . We called it the Tot Club. Well, I was one of the founders of this club, which is all over the United States and in different countries now.

Marion explains that her friends "were all very anxious for our children to know each other":

> In those days, you know, we were living far apart. Maybe in North Philadelphia or South Philadelphia or some up here [in Germantown]. My children were way up here. And maybe in West Philadelphia. Well, the only way we could bring them together we did it and had this meeting. . . . We're just used to being together. They were all first Philadelphians. . . . We just had like the Halloween parties and every first of the month we would meet at the Y and let the children play, you know, with games. Have souvenirs and games and things like that, for them to become acquainted.

This mothers' club quickly became a national social service organization devoted to bringing together upper- and middle-class African-American children. The Tot Club continues today as a nonprofit foundation devoted to social, education, and recreational projects for African-American children, with chapters in forty states. The club expanded rapidly in the 1940s and 1950s when segregation continued to compel African-American professionals to orient their practices and friendships around networks of other middle-class African-American families. Then, as now, the club has been criticized for its practices of excluding black mothers who were not personally sponsored, who were not light skinned, and who did not come from upper- and middle-class backgrounds. Marion herself is not happy about the formalizing of admission criteria:

> It just went bigger and bigger and bigger until it's really almost
> a political thing now. You've got to be registered by so many
> before you can enter it. Their names can be taken in through
> some of the members and so many of the members have to okay
> it or something.

It is the formalizing of entrance criteria that seems to have upset Marion. But as a young mother, she purposefully formulated the club as an exclusive group of high-status and economically advantaged families. Indeed, it was to tie her children to these other families that she upheld her relations to this collectivity of support.

It was within this context of socially exclusive networks that Marion forged her ties to medical discourse, and helped African-American physicians secure their professional practices and social position:

> Dr. Gary was Negro, Dr. Dickens, Dr. Alexander, Negro. So we
> tried to, uh, work with our people as much as we could, you
> know. After all, you wanted to give them work too, see. The
> others didn't have any trouble getting their work because as a
> rule it was more of them than it was of us. 'Cause I'm telling
> you when we first moved to North Philadelphia, it wasn't a
> colored person to be seen. When we saw a colored person go
> past the house we'd call all the rest of them and we'd peep, you
> know [laughs]. So that's why I'm saying that we tried to favor
> and help them because they're trying to get through life, the
> same way all other nationalities are, too.

In participating in these networks Marion saw herself as both having secured her ties to an advancing social group and gaining access to a network of protective caretakers. Her first child was delivered by Dr. Gary, "who came up and got me in the car, took me on to the hospital. I called him because we were very friendly. My brother was married to his cousin." Her second child was delivered by Dr. Dickens at the Aspiranto Health Home. I asked Marion why she moved from Gary to Dickens, and she answered by describing her relationships to these physicians:

> Well, because when I had [my first], Virginia [Alexander] was very upset. The Garys, see our family was intermingled there and I had just had Gary, you know and what not. But she was very upset, she said, "I thought I was suppose to deliver your first child?" So I says I'm gonna have another one and you can deliver that. And so when I got pregnant with the second one, I went to Virginia, she was tending me, you see. And that's how Helen Dickens delivered the child. When Virginia came back after leaving the room, she saw the baby and she sat down and cried, she said, "I missed the second one, didn't I?" I said, "Yes, but that's the end."

Dr. Dickens, she reports, later "gave my son [who went on to become a cardiologist] his first stethoscope."

Much like the Jewish women, the African-American women pursued their social-class mobility and aspirations as they constructed their domestic lives, orienting their activities toward forging network connections that marked and sustained their social position. Within these ties medicalization acquired its meaning.

There is an important contradiction here. Medicalization and the trappings of respectable motherhood united these women with the upwardly mobile Jewish women in their aspirations and ambitions. Yet their lives, mothering practices, and personal networks were entirely separate. Neither group went outside of its ethnoracial community for mothering advice. Medicalized mothering did not provide a basis for commonality, and, although its discourse was centered around a

purportedly objective science, in mothers' practices it served to reproduce and even expand social divisions among women already in place.

Medicalization was significant for these upwardly mobile and
community-oriented families for social as well as health reasons; it
served as a measure of social advance and helped to consolidate the ties
necessary for this advance. But medicalization was formulated in rela-
tional terms in yet another way as well; it developed in relation to the
practices of less-privileged African-American women for whom medicalization remained largely a frightening and remote prospect. The narratives of this latter group bring us to an entirely different discourse on
motherhood and medicalization, one centered as much around poverty
as medicine.

Chapter 6	"I Don't Know Any Doctors"

*Contradictions in Poor
and Working-Class
African-American
Mothers' Medicalization*

Unlike those of the upwardly mobile women, the working-class and working-poor African-American women's network ties immersed them in a mothering culture that was distant from expert discourse. These network relations were oriented toward everyday survival—meeting the daily pressures of maintaining paid work, providing for children, and managing with tight finances. Mothering in this context was a collective undertaking among women facing similar constraints, which weakened the desirability and possibility of orienting child care to the directives of medical discourse.

While their daily network ties around motherhood produced a culture of mothering that privileged the knowledge and routines of those in their immediate networks, these women were involved with other networks that presented an alternative model of motherhood, one forged in relation to expert discourse. These ties were typically with women (and occasionally men) in more privileged social-class and/or ethno-racial positions, such as white domestic employers for whom dominant medicine was at the center of their own mothering culture. Through these ties and models, working-class and poor African-American women were participants in but not insiders to the dominant, medically-oriented mothering culture. In these encounters we find again how the power of medical discourse works to sort and give meaning to women's relations to other women.

The Props of Medicalization: Time, Money, and Middle-Class Lives

In her analysis of how women's feeding work for their families is connected to dominant norms of motherhood, DeVault asserts that the dominant cooking discourse appears "class-neutral" (1991:200) but that the "class-neutral character of the image [of the good mother] obscures the crucial differences in the work of provisioning and in the different kinds of 'family' people are able to produce" (1991:201). Cooking discourse, which includes the texts as well as the social relations that produce them, presumes that all women live under the same circumstances and that they can freely choose to either accept or reject the recommendations, advice, and values of experts. In this illusion, differences among women are obscured (and typically pathologized), as are the constraints under which some women experience motherhood that might prevent them from adopting the codes of the dominant discourse. This is not insignificant for how constructions of "the good mother" are drawn in dominant codes; it is rarely the availability of resources that figures in the evaluation of mothering but the will, value, and motivation of individual women (Ladd-Taylor and Umansky 1998; Litt 1999).

Having the resources for constructing motherhood to meet dominant expectations was one of the underpinnings of middle-class women's medicalization. One of the striking aspects of the middle- and upper-middle-class women's narratives in my interviews is their representation of a seamless relationship to the expectations, demands, and rules of medical discourse. Women report in great detail their willingness to make their households and mothering routines amenable to medical dictates; only on rare occasions do these women mention having a difficult time making medical payments, keeping appointments, monitoring daily food intake, buying formula and food, or being able to locate and gain access to the physicians of their choice. Sue Thompson and Marion Marks discuss self-conscious struggles against racism in the medical establishment, which reveal a kind of seam between their lives and dominant medical practices. Yet we hear little about the difficulties they faced in shaping their households to the minutiae of medical demands. The actual work involved in accommodating medical requirements and the ability to carry them out—bending schedules, managing the different needs of others in the household, being available for monitoring children's activities—is left invisible in their narratives.

Barbara Schwartz, a Jewish middle-class woman for whom medicalization represented emergence into the middle class and "the American way," points to the importance of resources for her modern mothering culture, although she does not define them as such. Underneath the seamless picture of modern motherhood we find a series of props that enabled her to orient her mother work to medical protocols. Her description of her dual responsibility to run the family store and organize her children's care points to this adaptability:

> I ran up and down the steps [between the family's store and the apartment] to take care of the children. They'd leave school, they came in the store. You know, that sort of thing. We ate together and uh, I bathed them, I washed their hair and so on and all that I did. Every bit of it. I don't know how I did it.

This "up and down" was work that Barbara treasured, for it was her contention that the daily monitoring of and involvement in even the most mundane of child care activities was essential for her enactment of proper motherhood. Eating together, washing hair, monitoring homework, all constituted the successful carrying out of attentive motherhood. Unlike the women whose work schedules were not in their control and whose own household priorities were multiple and divided, Barbara was able to organize her daily routine in relation to her deeply felt priority of intensive mothering (Hays 1996). Undertaking activity directed toward her children defined the essence of good mothering.

Yet Barbara did not accomplish this household control alone; hiring housekeepers bolstered her capacity to do so. She employed domestic workers to perform "the menial work," diminishing the contradictions between working in the family pharmacy and her child care work, as she explains:

> I had a housekeeper and you know, they were with you a month or a week or whatever. You tried desperately to get some [help] not so much [to] help me with the children because I was with

the children. That's a very important thing. But I didn't have to do the menial work if I could get somebody. And that's what I wanted them to do.

According to historian Phyllis Palmer (1989), being able to divide the child care from, in Barbara's terms, "the menial work" was a measure of good motherhood in the 1930s and 1940s; mothers were warned by housekeeping experts that child care should be provided by mothers directly, not by servants, governesses, or domestics. Medical journals and popular health material also warned middle-class mothers that their skills and commitment were different from those of their "servants" and that they should try to keep their children from these uneducated and typically superstitious influences (Litt 1993). Thus, employing a housekeeper helped Barbara reduce her domestic workload at the same time that it signaled and helped her achieve her new status as a middle-class modern mother who took care of the children while a hired subordinate did the dirty work.

Barbara, like the other middle-class women, defining herself as a good, committed mother, implied that her mothering orientation was chosen, that it represented her style, learning, and skill (see also DeVault 1991). While giving her a basis for confidence as well as social acceptability, her perspective conceals the resources that made this style of mothering possible. What Barbara does not make explicit but what we can see is that there was a series of resources—money for a housekeeper so she would have more time and leniency in employment scheduling—that enabled her to pursue her mothering orientation.

In Barbara's narrative we see the features of motherhood that authorized mothers' representation of themselves as advanced and modern. The narratives obscure the significance of the material resources women drew on to meet the expectations embedded in their medicalized cultures. Because these resources are concealed, mothering is presented as free from the realities and constraints of everyday life. Women could make medicalized mothering appear effortless, although, as we saw, a great deal of work and many resources went into creating this appearance (Smith 1990).

Making Work Visible: Time, Money, and Poor Mothers' Lives

The women whose lives we examine below did not enjoy the resources that Barbara did. Their schedules were dominated by their wage work. Unlike Barbara, these women had little flexibility in organizing their daily timetables; they could not run up and down the stairs to wash their children's hair, plan a family meal, supervise a housekeeper—or even visit a gravely ill child in the hospital during working hours. In these families, managing paid work and child care defined the everyday reality of mothering.

Consider Jamie Rivers, a mother of eight children, who worked the evening shift, from 4:00 P.M. to midnight, doing cleaning work for a Philadelphia company. Her husband, who worked during the day, took responsibility for the children in the evening and night, as Jamie explains:

> Oh yeah, my husband did take care of my babies. . . . Yeah. I used to work one shift and he worked one shift. He take care of my baby at night. So he would come home and take care of my baby . . . 'til I come.

Jamie considered it her responsibility to coordinate the household work, preparing the food for the evening meals before she went to work. "Yes ma'am. Yeah. Make everything. Make the bottles, and everything. All he [my husband] had to do was just give it to [the baby]." Lucy Alston developed a similar routine. She worked as a domestic for a white family, cleaning and taking care of the children. For her own children's daily care, she relied on her kin and her husband, as she explains:

> I would take the children to [the] home [of a relative] that would be able to take care of them that day. And I'd take their lunch with them. And then my husband would, when he got off work, he would go get them and bring them home. And then he would give them their dinner if I had dinner prepared and if not he would fix something. But usually I'd always leave food ready for dinner when they got home.

Both Jamie and Lucy considered themselves the primary caregivers; it was up to them to coordinate various caretakers. And it is not surprising that it was in the preparation of meals that these women attempted to execute this control and responsibility, given the defining place of food preparation for the enactment of motherhood ideals (DeVault 1991). By providing this coordination work, Lucy and Jamie saw themselves as successfully executing their maternal responsibilities even in the face of challenges to it made by their employment as domestic workers for others (Rollins 1985).

The differences between Barbara's narrative and Jamie's and Lucy's point to very different possibilities for their relations to medical directives. The grinding details that the middle-class women took from medical directions, the scheduled feeding and sleeping, the measuring of food consumed, the exacting shopping requirements, and the continual medical appointments and supervision could only be met and valued as legitimate by mothers capable of at least approximating them. Beyond that, meeting medicalization's demands, as the middle-class women construct it, involved what Sharon Hays (1996) labels "intensive mothering," the idea and practice of exclusive, child-centered mothering. Middle-class women, with the supports of more available time, greater flexibility in their schedules, and solid finances, constructed their medicalized cultures in ways that sustained and produced the dominant model of mothering: the full-time, child-directed mother.

Dorothy Smith and Alison Griffith's (1990) analysis of the "sequencing" work that women perform to prepare their children for successful participation in school shows the middle-class presumptions about motherhood that are embedded in and rewarded through dominant institutional forms. Through interviews with mothers and analysis of school demands, Smith and Griffith conclude that school expectations of mothers' sequencing work assume a full-time stay-at-home mother available to monitor homework, meet with teachers, and adapt her schedule to those set by school officials. They refer to the discrepancy between schools' demands and nonnormative households (such as those with single mothers and employed mothers) as a "structural incompatibility" that puts particular pressures on mothers who are, then, constructed as deviant. One of the respondents in my study, Gloria Jones, provides an excellent example of the tension between expectations of a mother's availability and flexibility and the reality of her work life. Gloria's daughter, Jessie, was having trouble at school and Gloria was often called in to meet with the teachers. As a single, employed mother, however, Gloria was not available to report to school when the officials requested. To resolve this problem she asked her neighbor to help make sure that Jessie returned home from school on time. She also talked with her daughter about the importance of respecting her work schedule. In Gloria's words:

> I had a little problem when my daughter first started school. Because the kids used to . . . beat up on her and things, and she would come home crying and [the school] would call me on the job and I would go to school and I would say to her teacher, "Please, I'm trying to work and I can't if I have to get off of work and come over here. It's kind of hard for me." So the teacher said, "Well, after the kids leave school there's nothing they can do," which I imagine is true. So I told my daughter, I sat down and I talked to her again. I said, "Mommy has to work" and I said, "I have been having to get off for school all the time." I said, "I know it's pretty hard." . . . I told her "Sometimes you got to let the kids know that they can't just take advantage of you." So we talked about it. The next thing I know I didn't have no more problems there 'cause she started picking up for herself.

Fully aware of the conflict between her work schedule and the school's expectations, Gloria turned to her neighbor and daughter to help resolve the problem. It was up to her to establish this resolution; the school set its own routines and expectations with little regard for the interruptions and impossibilities they might create for employed mothers. In fact, the school legitimated the full-time, married, unemployed mother, because it was primarily these mothers who were available to meet school expectations. All mothers performed daily work to integrate their children into the school routines, but some women were better situated to make the adjustments required of this integration.

Medical rationales also presumed a similarity among household and mothering circumstances, and reinforced normative expectations about motherhood that appear socially neutral but actually reward and produce a very particular form of mothering. The ideals of mothering contained in medical discourse demanded a mother's daily monitoring, and time, money, and schedule flexibility. What we can see in the round of mothering that Lucy, Gloria, and Jamie describe is a daily practice that is organized around the edges of their employment demands. Managing child care in this context is not compatible with the availability implicitly demanded by medical discourse.

We see the seams between everyday life and medical discourse clearly in the mothering narratives of the single mothers. The nature of their everyday mothering shows a more intensified picture of reliance on personal networks for daily survival—and a distanced relation to medical discourse—than others, but the lessons from their lives are instructive. They show us what the process of forging ties to medical discourse looks like without the props of middle-class lives.

Daily Dependencies: Single Mothers and the Distance of Medicine

Nine of the African-American women in my study raised young children for at least some time without the presence of a male partner. Living without men's wages or even payments for child care left these women economically vulnerable. All worked for wages that were low. All except two were service or domestic workers. As we might expect, finances were extremely tight in their households, and much of their work as mothers was oriented toward filling the gaps left by insufficient financial resources, in part by daily reliance on other women for child care.

The single mothers developed extensive and indispensable relationships with women extending beyond the mother-child unit (Bell-Scott et al. 1991).[1] At some time, all of these women lived with relatives or "fictive kin" (Stack 1974) who shared child care responsibility. Ruth Cooper, for example, was divorced when her daughter was an infant. She reported that the time immediately following the separation was difficult, especially because her first cousin wanted the baby:

> People [say] "Give me that child. Give me that child." I said, "Uh-uh." That the harder time that I had [giving birth], I said, "I ain't giving nobody my child.". . . Some people did give their children away. But I ain't see about giving away no child myself. I said, "If I can have one, I can keep it."

Rather than give her baby away, Ruth brought her youngest sister in to live with them. She made a series of adaptive responses to the changes in her family circumstances, all of which were organized around and dependent on an extensive network of kin who moved in and out of each other's lives as the need for them arose.

Dixie Hann also describes a situation where conventional mother-child lines were blurred and a collective sense of caretaking prevailed. Dixie and her daughter, Bernice, lived with her sister and her sister's nine children. Dixie's sister worked at a coal camp in West Virginia. Because their own mother had died very early in their lives, Dixie had been raised by this elder sister, who then also helped to raise Bernice. Dixie explains the organization of caretaking:

> She's the one that raised me. . . . Yeah, I love my sister and I trusted my sister and you know, she raised me and she partly raised Bernice. Bernice crazy about my sister. She also call her mama. I call her mother [too].

Dixie describes an incident that depicts the shared work of raising the babies:

> You know, like babies, you know, get cramp in the stomach, like they have colic or something. And I had to turn her over to my sister then. . . . My sister come and get her from me and she would work on her.

Even before her baby was born, Dixie lived in her sister's household and helped with the children:

> 'Cause my sister's husband died when her baby [her youngest child] was about a year old. . . . I had to help my sister, you know, like raise her kids, get up bathe the kids, and at least comb the kids' heads to get to school. I had to help my sister raise her kids.

Dixie also cooked the dinners for everyone, "by time the kids get in from school, then I had the food done." Children were considered the shared responsibility of the women in the household. The division of labor was organized around the tasks that needed to be done rather than along formal mother-child lines.

Gloria Jones's changing domestic situation also had implications for her relations to medical discourse. After leaving her violent husband,

Gloria moved in with her stepfather and mother, where she provided the only income while they looked after Jessie, the baby. Her stepfather used traditional remedies and did not believe in doctors. She had little opportunity to consult a physician, for either herself or her child.

After yet another encounter with domestic violence—her stepfather hit her—Gloria moved into her own apartment. Her mothering practice changed. Among other things, she was free to cultivate ties to medicine now that she was out of the grip of her stepfather. Yet her employment demands, lack of money, and dependence on the other women in the apartment building to help care for her daughter defined her mothering practice. Gloria explains the organization of responsibility she shared with Miss Gertrude, her neighbor:

> And I met them [people in the building] when I moved in the apartment. They had a first, second, and third floor and everybody got to know, just like a big family in there. And so, she [Miss Gertrude] wasn't working. She had about, oh gosh, I think she had around five kids then and I told her, I said, "Would it be all right if Jessie went to school with one of [your] oldest kids?" I would get up in the morning and I'd make Jessie's breakfast . . . give her her breakfast. And I'd make her lunch and I gave the lady the key and I told her that Jessie's lunch would be upstairs. And she could come up there [to eat].

Gloria's dependence on her networks positioned her mothering differently in relation to medical norms. Mothering in this context was a collective undertaking among similarly situated households, which weakened the desirability and possibility of a mother's singular supervision of her children's feeding and other activities; network dependencies challenged the exclusive control of child care that we saw in middle-class women's medicalized narratives. For these reasons, the organization of child care was less private and less exclusive than for most middle-class married women who successfully crafted their mothering practices as part of a collectively valued discourse of modernization but at the same time were able, most often, to assert their independence in daily child care.

These African-American women's households did not often function as places of seclusion and separation from other households. Collins (1990) and Carothers (1990) identify the tradition of "other mothering" as providing resources to working-class and poor African-American women that mothers in dominant family forms do not enjoy. Black feminist scholarship on African-American motherhood contrasts "other mothering" with the dominant form of mothering described and criticized in white feminist scholarship (Hays 1996).[2] Carothers (1990) argues that the white feminist critique has focused on women's subordination to men in households, the denigration of their authority, and the psychological consequences of isolation. The constraints and racism that poor and working-class African Americans face distinguish them from the normative white middle-class woman in much white feminist scholarship. In the former, mothering occurs side by side with the real likelihood that, unmarried and in poorly paid occupations, the mothers will have to provide for their children in conditions of poverty or near poverty. Here, mothering is not a singular pursuit but a collective one among women, where borders are drawn not as much between individual men and women or households as between dominant white society and African Americans (Collins 1990).

In constructing child care as a shared responsibility, the single mothers I interviewed did not aspire to individual monitoring or control of children's everyday actions. We find here practices of mothering that were not organized to give primacy to medical discourse. Network dependencies and culture were not organized around shared participation in the modernizing discourse. Scientific authority was not presented as the final adjudicator of household conflicts. The social relations of caretaking these single mothers used both affirmed and produced their distance from dominant medical discourse. Rose Lyons's situation provides a good illustration of how daily life oriented toward managing the demands of paid work, few economic resources, and network dependencies could combine to create a reliance on networks that were not geared toward medicalization.

ROSE LYONS: POVERTY, NETWORKS, AND CHILD CARE

Oh, we ate good. But if anything was swallowed, then it
was good for you. Like I said, if you ate it and swal-
lowed it, it was good for him.

Rose Lyons

Born in 1911 in Virginia, Rose gave birth to her son, James, in 1932, when she was twenty-two. Rose's marriage dissolved after four years, a separation she said she initiated because of her husband's failure to provide for the family. She and James moved to a four-unit apartment building in a neighborhood she describes as "not beautiful, but, I'll put it this way, you didn't have to be afraid, you could have your door open, you know and you didn't have to worry or anything like that." Rose worked as a cook at a convalescent home, making "fifteen dollars for the first and the fifteenth," an appallingly low salary even by the standards of the 1930s. "It was hard, it was hard," Rose explained.

Not surprisingly, Rose oriented her mothering narrative around the financial problems she encountered and the everyday demands of managing paid work and child care. Much of her mothering work involved filling in the gaps between the shortage of money and her son's needs. Rose did not invoke medicalized language to describe her practices or her basis for knowledge. When I asked her how she knew to start her baby on solid food (a question itself reflecting a medical model), she said:

> Well, I'll tell you. If he didn't drink it, he didn't like it, he would not eat it. But I mean I tried to fix little things, the same thing that I fixed myself. But like take bread. I'd make biscuits like that for him and eat that. Or take something and make it, you know, make it look pretty or whatnot. Then he might probably eat it. But if it was something he really didn't like, he'd tell you, "I had some of that yesterday," that means he really did not like [it]. Now I'd never force him to eat anything he really did not like. But if anything was swallowed then it was good for you.

Rose's reliance on her son's "likes" and making his food "pretty" are approaches to feeding that did not appear in the middle-class women's accounts and certainly held no value in medical guidelines. For Rose, baby care was not a discrete activity organized around her child's particular eating needs or the advice of experts: her baby, as she says, "ate what I ate." Unlike the middle-class women, Rose did not speak of adjusting her household to meet the demands for scheduled and "staged" baby feeding made in medical discourse. Nor does she appear terribly invested in making the fit. "If he swallowed it," suggested Rose, "[it was] good for him."

When I asked Rose why she didn't go to the doctor for routine consultations, she invoked financial reasons as well as the sufficiency of her own strategies:

> Money's why. 'Cause what the doctor would charge you then you would need just the whole week. Food was very, very cheap then. I'm saying the days that he ate and I didn't have any more left over so, but I saw that he ate. I didn't eat.

Rose reveals a virtually unbridgeable gap between her everyday obligations and survival strategies and the expenses of medical intervention.

This gap reveals her dependence not on medical supervision but on her own judgment and knowledge. She explains that relying on a doctor for monthly checkups was simply out of the question. Home remedies, she insists, helped greatly:

> See, we couldn't go the doctor's every time anything happened when I was raising him. You went to the doctor but not every time, every little thing. You had to know things yourself. My mother did. My mother, she knew a lot of things. My mother would go out and get different things, you know, whatever different things was. [My grandmother] pulled us through when the flu was raging.

I asked her whether she used her grandmother's remedies as a mother herself:

> No. I mean you get away from these things. Know what I mean? You get modern, I guess. I mean you go and buy, you don't make, you don't bother with all these remedies. You go and buy.

Unlike the middle-class women, who expressed compulsion and desire in their movement toward becoming modern mothers, Rose characterized herself as relatively passive in relation to the changing terrain of medicine—"you get modern, I guess." Rose uses the second person, making reference to events around her, not to her own desire or will. She associates modern remedies with changing standards of household work and consumption but does not position herself at the center of these changes or even as welcoming them. Rose does not portray herself as an agent of technical or social progress; it was in reference to her own competence, strategies, and personal networks that she characterized herself as an agent and confident of her abilities.

Rose's connections with other women fostered this confidence and furthered her perception that medical rationales were unconnected to her circumstances. Her personal networks were not oriented toward medicalized contexts and they did not have access to private medical-care facilities and locally known and trusted physicians. Rose relied on these networks for child care as well as emotional and financial support; she called these networks a "family":

> I had nowhere to turn, [I] call them a family when they come to
> rescue without you asking, that is what I call a friend. Because
> sometime the burden it get so heavy that you cry and it's good
> to have a shoulder that you can lean on and tell your troubles to.

Rose depended on networks of women also for her daily household maintenance. As she explains, her "neighbor downstairs had a key and would turn the gas stove on [to heat the apartment], just before it was time for me to get home [from work], so it would be nice and warm in there." Another friend watched James while Rose worked. Rose described the exchange network she established with this friend, Ruth:

> Like if [Ruth] didn't have all of her rent or something like that,
> I would, you know, help. And I mean, different things, I mean,
> and she was sick, I mean I'd go out, be the one go to the
> hospital with her and all, to do her laundry, and things like
> that. I would do that for her because she couldn't do it. Because
> like I said she had that big tumor. And she would look after
> Jimmy, wasn't nothing but her looking after. She didn't have to
> dress him and nothing like that. He'd sleep home and I feed
> him. I mean I took care of those things like the only thing she
> had to do was just like give him his lunch. I'd give him his
> breakfast before leaving, and she'd give him his lunch.

Rose's approach can be distinguished from the "child-centered" one of the dominant middle-class model. Her household was part of a larger web of households, all contributing to the everyday survival of the others. And although Rose also establishes herself as the one responsible for meeting James's essential everyday needs of feeding, sleeping, and so on, she makes it very clear that it was these dependencies—these network relationships—that gave her a feeling of safety in raising her son: "Just for [Ruth] to be around and know he's safe. That was the most important thing."

Rose connects her dependence on Ruth to her economic deprivations, explaining that because there was

> somebody to look after my child, I would have a little bit left over so I could do it like that. You'd be surprised how you can stretch money when you have to. Phew. See, you don't know about that.

In labeling me as someone who could not understand serious money problems, Rose insists that her situation is best understood within her own networks. She draws distinctions between insiders and outsiders in her narration of mothering practices; here she positions herself as inside a close social circle of those excluded from economic stability and dominant medical practices.

Rose's narrative of managing the everyday contingencies of limited resources in the context of network interdependencies gives us a picture of medicalization that differs from those of women for whom household resources were ample. Like the other women in her circumstances, Rose gives priority to patching together a household routine that enabled her to maintain paid employment at the same time as care for her child. Her encounters with medicine were not smoothed over or protected by her social networks. Instead, these networks provided for her everyday survival and she in turn was indebted to them. Her interdependencies with networks provided a context for distance from medical discourse and they did little to instill her mastery over the massive medical complex that was surrounding her mothering practices.

Despite this system of caretaking, despite its departure from the normative ideal, and despite its lack of fit with medical directives, these women were exposed to the normative model and expectation of medically directed mothering. Medical discourse's unifying model, or what Dorothy Smith calls a "ubiquitous point of reference" (1990:175) for mothering, holds all women accountable despite the variety of settings and circumstances in which mothers actually live. It is in this contradiction that we see how medical discourse works as a dominant model for motherhood. It does not function simply as a set of textual directives. Rather, these women confront the normative power of medical discourse through relations with other women for whom medical discourse represents and enacts personal and collective advancement; relations with other women are "mediated by the standardization of . . . norms organized by this discourse" (Smith 1990:175). What is distinctive about this expert production of motherhood is not only that it renders some women inside the normative model and others outside, but that it produces how and with what meanings mothers enter into social relations with other women. In the middle- and upper-middle-class women's networks we have seen women cultivate relations to medicine among similarly positioned individuals, with essentially the same economic and social resources. But as we look at poor single mothers' relations to medical discourse we find another picture, one of difference among women rather than commonality.

Negotiating Difference

Poor African-American women forged ties to medical institutions and scientific advance without the supportive practices of middle-class networks or the resources enjoyed by more privileged families. These women encountered medical discourse in sites outside of their close networks, such as in hospitals during parenting lessons, in the homes of their domestic employers, in the doctors' offices where they worked; in sites, in other words, where their social status was marginal. It was through their employment and extended networks that these African-American women came into contact with others who worked within or had more access to medicine. Their "outsider-within" (Collins 1990) position gave them a perspective on medicalization that differed from that of women who believed in and worked for holding a central position in relation to medical institutions.

Just as the middle-class women discuss disparities in levels of care, these women focus on the differences between free city clinics, public hospital clinics, fee-for-service hospital clinics, family doctors, pediatricians, and so on; sorting through these varied institutional resources is very much at the center of their narratives. The attention to distinguishing between types of care reflects their marginal position; like Sue Thompson and Marion Marks, these mothers understand that race and class privileges were reproduced in the organization of the city's medical system. Sue describes the "stigma" and fear associated with Philadelphia General Hospital, where most African Americans received treatment:

> That place had a stigma out of this world. Oh, gosh, I mean, you were not supposed to come out of there if you went in there. I mean . . . it had all kinds of reputations not just that it was for poor and indigent people which of course had its own stigma. But it also [was] supposed to have been like a chop shop, I mean literally. People were given poor care there.

But unlike Sue and Marion, the poor African-American women were left to negotiate this medical system without a trusted and powerful network of other women and men.

Virtually none of these women could remember a physician's name, and only four had had more than passing contact with an individual physician. None used a physician within her family network. In developing their own connections to what they considered the best care possible, mothers enhanced their children's health as they negotiated their "outsider-within" position relative to the dominant medical system.

Celia McNeil, for example, rejected the free city clinic in favor of the "paying" hospital clinic, a response to the death of her son that she attributes to poor treatment he received at the free clinic. Her description of the tragedy speaks to the distance she felt from the medical establishment as well as to her determination to find the right kind of care, as we see:

> This [death] is because I wasn't experienced at all with children. My first one, and I was only nineteen. Well, when he was born I took him back to clinic, just like I was supposed. He had all of his needles and whenever I had an appointment I was there. Now he had an appointment for a Wednesday. I'll never

forget it. And I took him in because he had had a cold. And
when I had him home then, when he would cough, he would
choke. So I told the doctor, this was a woman doctor. . . . She
told me "Oh, just hold his head down like this and put some
nose drops in his nose." That was the extent of the examination. She didn't listen to his chest, she didn't undress him or do
anything. Uh, what hurt me was there was a lady there that had
a little girl and she had just come from the hospital. She had
had pneumonia. She was coming to the clinic and this doctor
undressed her, and examined her all over. Now this child had
just been discharged from the hospital, mine had never been. I
could never understand why she didn't do mine . . . take my
baby and examine him.

Celia changed her practices of seeking medical care for her children
after that incident as well as her relation to medical personnel, as she
explains:

I knew better anyway. I knew what to say, how to . . . ask and
what to do. . . . I didn't have any problem after that first one.
That was the experience I learned from. I knew what to say and
I never took them to another clinic. I took them to the doctor.
Doctor would know the child because in the clinics you go this
week and you'll have a doctor and the next time you go and
you have a different doctor. And they don't always read the
charts. So when I had my next children I said, "No more
clinics."

Celia then turned to the "paying" clinic at the hospital:

I took them to the hospital clinic. No more free clinics. No
more city clinics. [It was] much better. I figure, you'd pay
something, you get a little bit more service. After that all the
doctors that I took the children to they all had the same doctor.

The family doctor, she explained, "knew us all, he knew each one of
us" and "when you go in and you have a doctor like that, he ask you
about the one that's not there. How is your husband doing, what's this,
what's that?" What Celia's narrative reveals, which was very typical
among these women, was the awareness of disparity in medical care,
even a belief that she was a victim of medical malpractice.

The mothers worked to secure what they considered better medical care for their children; many did this through relations with whites who had more access to and familiarity with the medical system. We find here a kind of mirroring of the exclusivity that middle-class women developed in and through their segregated medicalized cultures; these women cultivated ties that connected them to others outside of their ethnoracial and social-class group.

In her memoir of being "a white mother of Black sons," Jane Lazarre explores the daily negotiations of race and racism embedded in her cross-racial mothering, one aspect of which is recognizing her own privilege and power in relation to her sons, husband, and in-laws. At one point in her narrative she speaks to her own racial power as something her black mother-in-law, Lois, uses to get medical attention in an emergency room:

> In . . . matters of race consciousness and Black pride, of wariness and readiness of battle, Lois' ability to win out over fate and survive dire social conditions, are famous. Once, waiting for admission to an emergency room when Simeon [Lois's son] was sick, she told me bluntly: "Go tell them we've been here for hours. They'll believe you cause you're white." She is a resistance fighter at heart and by necessity. I obey her, resent her, tease her, am angry or grateful or frustrated and always full of admiration. (1996:106)

After many years of witnessing, participating in, and learning in this community of resistance, the "life stories" of her black kin come to influence Lazarre as well, and shape a new identity for her. Yet when the African-American women in my study borrowed the power of white privilege just as Lois did, these were not occasions for forging collective identities. Rather, these were experiences of temporary alliance organized more by differences than by coming together across an otherwise divided motherhood.

Many women turned to friends' employers, co-workers, bosses, or landlords who offered a link to this important but hard to control resource of modern medicine, especially when their children were ill. For childbirth, for example, Gloria used the obstetrician for whom her mother did domestic work; Blanche Pierce decided that vaccinations and other medical advances were important after learning that her sister's employer, "the first [person] to receive insulin," had benefited from new medical knowledge. These women encountered the advances and benefits of medicine in arenas outside their closest network ties. Instead of a celebration of collective social mobility we find in the working-class women's narratives a personal struggle with unsatisfactory care and lack of power in relation to medical establishments and personnel.

Cheryl O'Neil's narrative of forging connections to better medical care through others who had more economic and social power shows how the power of medical discourse develops in the context of women's differences from one another. She learned of the status of dominant medicine for child care while she worked as a domestic for a white employer who used pediatricians. Because she saw her employers as "schooled" people, Cheryl decided that she too would pursue the use of a private doctor rather than the clinic, as she explains:

> I was doing housework and child care, taking care of people's children. And a lot of the people I would work for used 'em. They were schooled, maybe doctor, lawyer, something like that. And that's what I did. So I found me one. I looked in the Yellow Pages and found one closest to me, and [if] the name sounded good, [I went].

Cheryl never spoke directly with her employers about this decision; she simply followed the example her employer set. Here we see the distance between domestics and their employers from the perspective of the employee. It was on her own terms—with her own scant resources—that Cheryl switched from free to paid services, with the belief that she would get better care for her children. She became so convinced of the superiority of private, paid care that she worked longer hours and sacrificed other purchases:

> I had a medical card. I didn't use it. I took my money out of work for it and paid [for] the [doctor]. I figured that they wouldn't . . . give you the right stuff [with the medical card] because they were giving you something. I would work extra hours to make extra money, make sure that I paid for it. So my [children], they got top-notch everything. When I stopped going to the hospital, to the regular clinic, I had a private

pediatrician for them to go to. I will always get baby doctors. I will always find me one somewhere.

Like others who came to identify the advantages of private medical care through the model of their employers, Cheryl copied the practice of her more privileged employer but did so without the resources or advantages they enjoyed; in her case, also without the help of the employer or the use of their doctor. Working twelve hours a day, commuting from the central city to the suburbs, taking care of her employer's children while her own were looked after by others, all point to the limits of structuring her relation to medical discourse in the terms her employer could adopt. In seeking private medical care Cheryl identified with these more privileged women; in this identification Cheryl pictured herself as carrying out the kind of mothering she respected in her employers. Yet without the social networks and artifacts of status mobility that her employers enjoyed, hers was an approach to medical discourse that approximated but could not reproduce the medicalized mothering of the middle class.

Shirley Elliot's experience of dealing with a gravely ill son captures many of the themes of these women's "outsider-within" position to a medicalized culture of motherhood. Shirley raised her children in a house that she shared with her husband and "Miss Helen." One morning Shirley's son, Edgar, came downstairs and said, "Mama, God came for me last night," a foreboding sign of his death, according to Shirley. She explains her response:

> I said [to Edgar], "Let's go down there and tell Miss Helen that."
> And [Miss Helen] said, "We'd better take him to a doctor." I
> said, "I don't know any doctors." So she took me to her doctor.
> And he examine him and said that, he gave me a prescription
> to get the medicine and he said that to give him this. The
> direction was on the bottle. And he would be all right. And
> [Edgar] began to get worse and worse until I didn't take him
> back to that doctor.

Not being satisfied with the results, she found herself desperate for a new approach. Shirley explained the problem to her landlord, who responded by bringing over his own physician:

The owner of the house, he said, "Let my doctor try you." He
was a Jewish man. And [the doctor] would come, you know,
and give him medicine, examine [him]. But seemed like wasn't
none of the medicine doing any good. And he was charging, I
think it was eighteen dollars a week. . . . And one day the
landlord said to him, he said, "Now how could anybody living
in a little place like this pay eighteen dollars a week," he said to
the doctor. So then he cut it down to twelve dollars a week.
Well, I had a few pennies in the bank then. But I would draw it
out, you know, and pay him.

Shirley's landlord acted as an advocate and carried out the initial contact and price negotiation with the physician; he was able to because
he was closer in status than Shirley was to the physician. But still, Edgar
did not improve. Shirley then decided to try to get her son admitted to
the hospital where her sister worked as a housekeeper:

See now, his temperature wouldn't ever go down. And this
doctor he didn't know what to do. And so one day, I went in
there. I thought he was dying. Looked [to] me he was dying. I
went downstairs and told Helen, I said, "Edgar's dying." . . .
And the doctor came. I sent for the doctor. And the doctor said
that his temperature had gone down. But he didn't see that so
much different . . . in him. . . . And so but he said that he didn't
know anything that he could do. And so I asked him, I said,
"Will it be all right if I take him over to this hospital?" He said,
"If you can it will be good." See I had a sister who worked [at
the hospital]. And so I called her and asked her if I brought him
over there to put him in the hospital, it will be all right. She
said yeah, but give her address. So I did. You had to live there
in [that part of town to get admitted].

In Shirley's situation we see a typical example of women marshaling
whatever connections and resources they could to gain access to the
medical treatment they deemed essential. Such multiple moves, from
one health system to another and one health provider to another, were
more common for women who were outsiders to the medical establishment than for the middle-class women. In this case, the moves were
central to a son's survival. Without personal connections to help them

navigate the system, these women found themselves inviting help from varied, and often distant, contacts.

It is appropriate here to return to my comment in the introduction about the tension I felt in my interviews with working-class African-American women, to whom I was a symbol of medical expertise, of dominant motherhood, around which they felt judged, and in relation to which they constructed themselves as outsiders. A number of women were exasperated at my continued questioning. Lucy stated that the interview was "beginning to get on her nerves." Another woman, as I was leaving, said "I've got a story for you," and told me, as I was halfway down the hall heading to the elevator, about her father's treatment during slavery. A third woman said that she didn't "have a hard luck story like [I] might expect." One woman hugged me when I told her I was Jewish, proclaiming our mutuality because she had worked as a domestic for a Jewish family and learned to cook "Jewish foods." Clearly, much was at stake in our interaction because of our different positions in relation to the dominant discourse. Here was a lesson in how our separate relations to this discourse were enacted and understood as differences between us as women; it was not to, or through, the discourse itself that we were reacting, but to each other as representatives of different sides of it.

Conclusion

In the terms set out by social reformers and medical professionals, the ethic of scientific motherhood held great promise for the improvement of everyday life. Just as technological advances in industrial work and transportation were apparently enriching the public domain, the advances of science and medicine were seen to benefit the most ordinary of daily activities. As infant mortality and morbidity improved and as childhood diseases became less life-threatening, medical attention turned increasingly to the healthy child, with physicians defining themselves as "counselors of health." The scientific supervision of child care came to depend on a new approach to motherhood, one that required women's admission of their own ignorance and their interest in cultivating ties to the modernizing era around them. Scientific motherhood advocates looked to a strong link between mothers and experts in order to improve the lives of innocent and vulnerable children.

Yet these advocates, physicians among them, promised more than good health. They also endorsed the idea of a community of mothers, a unified motherhood, that science held the potential to create. From the maternalist reformers in the 1910s and 1920s to the medical experts in the 1930s and 1940s, science was offered as a counter to the ethnoracial and class diversity of mothering practice. As a modern ideology of assimilation, the ethic of scientific motherhood was particularly appealing because it provided a solution to the divisions permeating American society.

And yet, women of diverse social positions constructed scientific motherhood very differently. Jews and African Americans developed socially homogenous practices, formal and informal, for educating mothers and improving family life, practices that secured and reflected class and ethnoracial segregation. Some women had more access than others to the information and technologies of medical discourse. Women who grew up in the South and who raised their children there had virtually no contact with professionals, only to be introduced to them in the profoundly life-changing experience of migration. Upwardly mobile Jewish women who lived in immigrant households looked to medicine as a sign of social acceptance and inclusion, while African-American upper-middle-class women saw in medicine a site of both their exclusion from white society and the promise of collective struggle to dismantle white privilege. Working-class and poor African-American mothers were more likely to cross class and ethnoracial lines, but did so not as part of a collectively advancing social group but in conditions of continued marginality to these groups.

The power of medical discourse, while institutionalized in government programs and formal rhetoric, was also produced in contexts beyond medical settings. Medicalization's power as a regulatory discourse of everyday life is evident in women's relations with each other. For middle- and upper-middle-class women, medicalization meant establishing and promoting economically and ethnoracially homogenous communities, ones that explicitly and implicitly excluded women of other social-class and ethnoracial positions. Beyond that, upwardly mobile women's networks also forged and depended on ties to men in these networks. In these contexts, medicalization was a collectively held strategy for social and economic advance, in which becoming a normatively acceptable mother was tied to socially homogenous and segregated ties. While these socially segregated ties facilitated women's embrace and incorporation of modern motherhood as well as social-class mobility, they did little to encourage mothers to cross ethnoracial or class boundaries. Medicalization may not have been a single cause of differences among women, but it was a site where difference and commonality were clearly executed and produced.

African-American poor and working-class women employed different strategies of social advance, rooted in networks of women who also had limited financial and domestic flexibility and who were not connected to medicalized networks and institutions. Their everyday lives were structured around ties with women much like themselves. These women engaged with medical discourse largely through contacts with women, and occasionally men, with more social power and privilege than themselves. This did not signal collective status mobility. Their tentative, outsider relation to medicalized motherhood (and medicalized mothers) placed these women outside the bounds of modern motherhood, where they came to represent a model of socially devalued motherhood. Their fear of criticism is not far from the surface in their accounts.

Women's relationship to medicalization positions them differently in relation to dominant cultural ideals. The development and maintenance of standards of motherhood are inextricably connected to the distribution of power and authority in society (Mullings 1997). All of these women stood at some distance from the dominant cultural values of motherhood. Nonetheless, the middle-class women helped create and sustain standards of motherhood against which the practices of women like Shirley, Rose, and Gloria had even less chance of appearing normative and acceptable.

The processes of medicalization are far from straightforward. Medical rhetoric aside, the processes through which medical authority made its way into mothers' households were not a neutral, progressive march of science. My goal in this book has been to redirect our thinking about medicalization away from a perspective that assumes, however implicitly, either women's common victimization by medicalization or that women commonly accepted medicine's premises on its own scientific terms. Rather, women's use of medical discourse made medicalization yet another social institution that reproduced ethnoracial exclusions and barriers.

Gender was divided in medicalization; women's medicalized cultures constructed divisions not only between men and women, but also among women themselves. The practice of medicalization linked women to an ideal of social and cultural homogeneity. In its daily practice, middle-class motherhood privileged unity over diversity. And in creating motherhood through constructions of sameness, these women in my sample defined borders around their communities which undermined the possibilities for understanding mothering from other perspectives, invited women to distance themselves from mothers and children un-like themselves, and cultivated self-evaluation and censure. The case of the poor and working-class African-American mothers who aspired to follow the practices of white middle-class women throws the tenac-ity of these divisions into sharp relief; although sharing aspirations for their children's health, in practice their medicalized motherhoods did nothing to bring these women together (even in dialogue) across the racial and class divide. Instead of establishing links across race, ethnicity, and class, medicalization cemented social divisions, bringing these into greater relief and giving them new, scientifically justified resilience.

Iris Young's critique of the ideal of community sheds light on the dangers that the ideal of homogeneity can hold for motherhood:

> Community is an understandable dream, expressing a desire for
> selves that are transparent to one another, relationships of
> mutual identification, social closeness and comfort. The dream
> is understandable, but politically problematic, I argue, because
> those motivated by it will tend to suppress differences among
> themselves or implicitly to exclude from their political groups
> persons with whom they do not identify. (1990:300)

The desire for unity and the inevitability of divisiveness create a ten-sion that has a long history in feminist thought on motherhood. The potential of motherhood to forge alliances among otherwise differently situated women has been a long cherished ideal among some feminists (largely white), dating back to the maternalists. In her study of femi-nist ideas of motherhood, Lauri Umansky (1996) notes that, while never voicing the dominant discourse, white cultural feminist scholars and activists in the early 1980s foregrounded motherhood as a universaliz-ing issue, as an arena where feminists, divided by debates about sexuality and race, could come together and forge a unilateral critique of patri-archy. The promise of motherhood, for feminism and for a new ethic of social life, was embedded in the female ethic of caring that mothers constructed in their caretaking (Chodorow 1978; Gilligan 1982; Ruddick 1982). Yet here, too, the desire for a universal discourse and common identity both hides and furthers inequalities already in place. Rather than forging a common identification, the very desire for unifi-cation reflects and constructs borders and exclusions.

It might seem a long way around to end a study of scientific motherhood with a discussion of difference and inequality among women and feminists. Yet this is precisely how science has been taken up, never far from debates about and constructions of difference, of the good and the bad mother. Today that debate is focused on linking purportedly genetic difference to social worth (Rothman 1998). The disproportionate targeting of African-American and Hispanic pregnant women in the campaign against substance abuse during pregnancy is yet another recent example of the tie between ethnoracial difference and medical discourse. Here we find a new alleged bad mother (re)producing the next generation of delinquents (Litt and McNeil 1997). The current round of welfare reform similarly draws on expert portrayals of the so-called pathology of women on welfare. These are debates that are framed by scientific discourse but taken up in everyday life, by courts, policemen, news reporters, hospital personnel, and women carrying out their lives as mothers. And it is in the everyday use that mothers make of expert knowledge to construct evaluations among themselves that we find the clearest proof of that discourse's power in constructions of motherhood.

There is much more work to be done to unpack the associations among social inequality and medical authority outlined in this book. Important questions remain: In which circumstances do motherhood practices challenge the association between medical authority and social divisions? In what contexts do women use expert discourse to come together across difference and how is this sustained? With these questions in mind we can return to my cousin Bessie, whose belief in modern medical science supported her own sense of distance from "tribalness" and other mothers, whose situations she knew nothing about and with whom she had no personal contact. It is precisely this form of social relation that has become embedded in the dominant mothering discourse. Bessie's participation in the discourse—even a generation later—mediated her relations to the women she heard about, and her evaluations of their competence and authority. If she had given herself a moment to think, Bessie surely would have suppressed her sense of maternal superiority, but the divided character of modern motherhood, whether articulated or suppressed, is a social reality.

Appendix   Biographical Profiles

Alston, Lucy. b. 1909, North Carolina. African American. Two children, first born in 1933 or 1934. Married in 1933.

Brown, Diana. b. 1916, Philadelphia. Jewish. Two children, first born in 1939. Married in 1937.

Cohen, Selma. b. 1918, Philadelphia. Jewish. Two children, first born in 1940. Married in 1938.

Cooper, Ruth. b. 1908, North Carolina. African American. One child, born in 1950. Married. Separated after childbirth.

Elliot, Shirley. b. 1906, North Carolina. African American. Two children, first born in 1943. Married in 1930. Husband died in 1961.

Epstein, Sylvia. b. 1905, Philadelphia. Jewish. One child, born in 1931. Married in 1929. Husband died when daughter was in late teens.

Franks, Clara. b. 1919, North Carolina. African American. Eight children, first born in 1938. Married in 1937 or 1938.

Goldschmidt, Essa. b. 1910, Russia. Jewish. Three children, first born in 1928. Married in 1927.

Hann, Dixie. b. 1930, Alabama. African American. One child, born in 1946 or 1947. Married sometime after 1963. Husband died in 1972.

Hannah, Carrie. b. 1916, York, Pennsylvania. African American. Three children, first born in 1938. Never married.

Harris, Vivian. b. 1909, Russia. Jewish. Two children, first born in 1934. Married in 1932.

Herbert, Mary. b. 1929, Georgia. African American. One child, born in 1942. Married in 1948. Separated in 1952.

Herbert, Reather. b. 1918, North Carolina. African American. Sixteen children, first born in 1935. Never married.

Horowitz, Sadie. b. 1918, Philadelphia. Jewish. Two children, first born in 1944. Married in 1941.

James, Mildred. b. 1908, North Carolina. African American. Three children, first born in 1925. Married in 1924. Husband died in 1929 or 1930.

Jones, Gloria. b. 1911, Florida. African American. One child, born in 1928. Married in 1928. Left husband in 1932 or 1933 and divorced him.

Kleiner, Rose. b. 1911, Philadelphia. Jewish. Two children, first born in 1938 or 1939. Married in 1932.

Kleinman, Judith. b. 1909, Philadelphia. Jewish. Three children, first born in 1930. Married in 1929.

Levin, Edna. b. 1918, Brooklyn, New York. Jewish. Two children, first born in 1946. Married.

Lyons, Rose. b. 1911, Virginia. African American. One child, born in 1932. Married. Separated in 1935.

Marks, Marion. b. 1909, South Carolina. African American. Two children, first born in 1934. Married in 1930.

McNeil, Celia. b. 1917, Philadelphia. African American. Four children, first born in 1936. Married in 1935.

Miller, Esther. b. 1920, Philadelphia. Jewish. Two children, first born in 1941. Married in 1940.

O'Neil, Cheryl. b. 1924, North Carolina. African American. Five children, first born in 1939. Married in 1942. Husband left when she was pregnant with son, 1960 or 1961 and they divorced.

Pierce, Blanche. b. 1915, Philadelphia. African American. Seven children, first born in 1933. Married twice; first marrriage was in the early 1930s.

Ragowitz, Lori. b. 1919, Philadelphia. Jewish. Three children, first born in 1944. Married in 1941.

Reisner, Elsie. b. 1894, Philadelphia. Jewish. Three children, first born in 1920. Married in 1919.

Rivers, Jamie. b. 1916, North Carolina. African American. Eight children, first born 1930 or 1931. Married in 1929.

Rosenfeld, Sarah. b. 1914, Philadelphia. Jewish. Three children, first born in 1937 or 1938. Married in 1931.

Rubin, Mimi. b. 1917, Lansdale, Pennsylvania. Jewish. Three children, first born in 1940. Married in 1938.

Schwartz, Barbara. b. 1911 or 1912, Philadelphia. Jewish. Two children, first born in 1939. Married in 1937 or 1938.

Sein, Estelle. b. 1913, Russia. Jewish. Three children, first born in 1932. Married in 1930.

Sheppard, Brenda. b. 1898, South Carolina. African American. Fourteen children, first born in the 1920s. Married. Husband died when children were young.

Steinberg, Abby. b. 1925, Philadelphia. Jewish. One child, born in 1945. Married in 1943.

Taylor, Phyllis. b. early 1920s, North Carolina. African American. Two children, first born in the 1940s. Married in the late 1930s or early 1940s.

Thompson, Sue. b. 1930, Philadelphia. African American. Two children, first born in 1954. Married in 1950.

Weinberg, Diane. b. 1910, Philadelphia. Jewish. One son, born in 1939. Married.

Woodall, Tessie. b. 1911, South Carolina. African American. Two children, first born in 1943 (niece's daughter). Married in 1948. Husband had six-year-old son.

Notes

Introduction

1. The terms *race* and *ethnicity* have had varied definitions in scholarly and popular writing throughout this century (Brodkin 1998; Frankenberg 1993; Omi and Winant 1994). The term *ethnicity* came into use largely after the Second World War and emphasized that cultural attributes rather than biological ones define a people or nation. In the later part of the twentieth century, *ethnicity* is being used to refer to the cultural heritage of Europeans while *race* is being used to refer to non-Europeans. Jews and African Americans have been described through both "racial" and "ethnic" markers. Because the meanings of *ethnicity* and *race* have shifted throughout the century and because they share a common sociohistorical pattern of demarcating social identity and assignment, I follow Brodkin's (1998) lead and collapse these terms into the adjective *ethnoracial* to describe both Jews and African Americans. At times I also use *race* and *ethnicity*, and mean them to be understood interchangeably.
2. See also Arnup 1994; Davin 1978; Deacon 1985; Donzelot 1979; Grant 1998; Jones 1983; Ladd-Taylor and Umansky 1998; Walzer 1998; Walkerdine and Lucey 1989.
3. See also Avery 1990; Collins 1999; Davis 1981; Fraser 1998; Harding 1993; McBride 1989; Rydell 1993; Smith 1995.
4. The names of all the respondents and, except when noted, of all the physicians are fictitious, as is the name of the Tot Club (chapter 5).
5. See also Beoku-Betts 1995; DeVault 1991; DiLeonardo 1984; Edwards 1990; Etter-Lewis and Foster 1996; Fraser 1998; Geiger 1986; Rapp 1990; Reissman 1987; Rosenwald and Ochberg 1992; Shopes 1994; Stacey 1994; Toth 1989; Wheatley 1994a and 1994b.
6. See also Avery 1990; Fraser 1998; Giddings 1984; Logan 1989; McBride 1989.
7. See also Joeres and Laslett 1993; Mechling 1975; Smith 1993; Stivers 1993; Toth 1989; Yans-McLaughlin 1990.

Chapter 1   Scientific Motherhood

1. See also Arnup 1994; Grant 1998; Halpern 1988; Jones 1983; Tomes 1997.
2. See also Kuznick 1994; Marchland 1985; McClary 1980; Merchant 1980; Newman 1985; Rubin 1983; Rydell 1993; Starr 1982.
3. See also Arnup 1994; Berch 1980; Cowan 1983; Davies 1988; Davin 1978; Deacon 1985; Ehrenreich and English 1979; Fox 1990; Grant 1998; Holt 1995;

Hobbs 1988; Jones 1983; Ladd-Taylor 1986, 1994; Schlossman 1976; Shapiro 1986; Sklar 1973; Stage and Vincenti 1997; Tomes 1997.

4. See also Cowan and Cowan 1989; Ewen 1985; Glenn 1990; Meckel 1990; Rose 1994; Weinberg 1988.

5. See also Apple 1987, 1995; Ladd-Taylor 1986; Meckel 1990; Rothman 1978; Smith 1995; Weiss 1977, 1978.

6. See also Halpern 1988; Leavitt 1986.

7. See also Clarke 1998; Davis-Floyd and Dumit 1998; Fraser 1998; Martin 1992; Markens et al. 1997; Mink 1995; Petchesky 1990; Strathern 1992.

8. See also Apple 1987, 1995; Arnup 1994; Grant 1998; Jones 1983; Litt 1993, 1996, 1997; Theriot 1993; Tomes 1997; Walzer 1998.

9. See also Abel 1995, 1996; Arnup 1994; Franklin and Ragoné 1998; Fraser 1998; Grant 1998; Ladd-Taylor 1986; Leavitt 1986; Martin 1992, 1994a, 1994b; McNeil 1988.

10. See also DeVault 1991; Grant 1998; Walzer 1998.

11. See also Bell-Scott et al. 1991; Boris 1993; Carby 1987; Collins 1990; Dill 1994; Harley 1988; Ladd-Taylor and Umansky 1998; Lazarre 1996; Litt 1999; Polakow 1993; Scheper-Hughes 1992; Sidel 1986; Walkerdine and Lucey 1989.

Chapter 2 *"I Was a Modern Mother"*

1. See also Baum et al. 1976; Ewen 1985; Friedman-Kasaba 1996; Glenn 1990; Heinze 1990; Joselit 1994.

2. See also Baum et al. 1976; Brodkin 1998; Goldstein et al. 1993; Joselit 1994; Moore 1981; Weinberg 1988.

3. See also Baltzell et al. 1983; Hershberg et al. 1979; Rosen 1983; Tabak 1990; Whiteman 1973.

4. See Apple (1987) and Halpern (1988) for detailed descriptions of the daily regimen required by the new model of well-baby care.

Chapter 3 *"My Mother Was with Me All the Time"*

1. See also Afro-American Historical and Cultural Museum 1990; Clark-Lewis 1994; Gates 1993; Hine 1996; Jones 1985; Lemke-Santangelo 1996; Lewis 1996; Phillips 1996.

2. See also Clark-Lewis 1994; Gates 1993; Jones 1985; Lemke-Santangelo 1996; Lewis 1996; Marks 1989; Phillips 1996.

3. The data on which the Tanner family's story is based was collected during an interview I had with the daughter of the family, Sue Thompson. This was the only occasion in the book where I use the reflections of a child of migrants. Because of their unique socioeconomic situation, it is useful to see these reflections in the context of social mobility and medicalization.

4. According to McNeil Consumer Products Company, the distributor of Tylenol, it was 1961 when regular-strength Tylenol was first introduced and 1975 when Extra Strength came on the market. The first Tylenol to be distributed (with a prescription) was in 1955, when McNeil introduced the acetaminophen elixir for children (McNeil Consumer Products 1999). Clearly, each of these dates was later than the period when Jamie actually raised her young children, so Extra Strength Tylenol was not relevant to her mother work. What we find in her comment is a conflation of medical with pharmaceutical technology. More to the point, we see a running-together of techniques that are not consonant

with her experience in the South: what aligns "extra Tylenol" with doctors' and nurses' orders is their remoteness from her daily life.

Chapter 6 **"I Don't Know Any Doctors"**

1. See also Carothers 1990; Collins 1990; Davis 1981; Giddings 1984; Gordon 1994; Harley 1988; Stack 1974; Vrettos 1989.
2. See also Bell-Scott et al. 1991; Carothers 1990; Collins 1990; Davies 1985; Davis 1981; Giddings 1984; Harley 1988; Stack 1974.

Bibliography

Abel, Emily K. 1995. "A 'Terrible and Exhausting' Struggle: Family Caregiving during the Transformation of Medicine." *Journal of the History of Medicine and Allied Sciences* 50:478–506.

———. 1996. "Appealing for Children's Health Care: Conflicts between Mothers and Officials in the 1930s." *Social Service Review* 70:282–304.

———. 1998. "Hospitalizing Maria Germani." In *"Bad" Mothers: The Politics of Blame in Twentieth-Century America*, ed. by Molly Ladd-Taylor and Lauri Umansky. New York: New York University Press.

Abraham, Laurie Kaye. 1993. *Mama Might Be Better Off Dead: The Failure of Health Care in Urban America*. Chicago: University of Chicago Press.

Afro-American Historical and Cultural Museum. 1990. *"Let This Be Your home": The African American Migration to Philadelphia, 1900–1940*. Brochure. Philadelphia: Afro-American Historical and Cultural Museum.

Alexander-Minter, Rae. 1986. Speech given at the unveiling of a portrait of Virginia Alexander. Medical College of Pennsylvania Hahnemann University. Archives and Special Collections on Women in Medicine.

Alston, Marilyn Baker. 1987. "Historic Health-Related Benefits for Black Philadelphians." Master's thesis, Temple University School of Social Work, Philadelphia.

Apple, Rima D. 1987. *Mothers and Medicine: A Social History of Infant Feeding, 1890–1950*. Madison: University of Wisconsin Press.

———. 1995. "Constructing Mothers: Scientific Motherhood in the Nineteenth and Twentieth Centuries." *Social History of Medicine* 8(2):161–178.

Arnup, Katherine. 1994. *Education for Motherhood: Advice for Mothers in Twentieth-Century Canada*. Buffalo, N.Y.: University of Toronto Press.

Ash, Rachel. 1930. "That Zest for Food." *Hygeia* 8:916–917.

Avery, Byllye Y. 1990. "Breathing Life into Ourselves: The Evolution of the National Black Women's Health Project." In *The Black Women's Health Book: Speaking for Ourselves*, ed. by Evelyn C. White. Seattle: Seal Press.

Baca Zinn, Maxine. 1994. "Feminist Rethinking from Racial-Ethnic Families." In *Women of Color in U.S. Society*, ed. by Maxine Baca Zinn and Bonnie Thornton Dill. Philadelphia: Temple University Press.

Baltzell, E. Digby, Allen Glicksman, and Jacquelyn Litt. 1983. "The Jewish Communities of Philadelphia and Boston: A Tale of Two Cities." In *Jewish Life in Philadelphia 1830–1940*, ed. by Murray Friedman. Philadelphia: ISHI Publications.

Banner-Haley, Charles Pete T. 1993. *To Do Good and To Do Well: Middle-Class Blacks and the Depression, Philadelphia, 1929–1941*. New York: Garland Publishing.

Baum, Charlotte, Paula Hyman, and Sonya Michel. 1976. *The Jewish Woman in America*. New York: Dial Press.

Beardsley, Edward. 1987. *A History of Neglect: Health Care for Blacks and Mill Workers in the Twentieth-Century South*. Knoxville: University of Tennessee Press.

Bell-Scott, Patricia, Beverly Guy-Sheftall, Jacqueline Jones Royster, Janet Sims-Wood, Miriam DeCosta-Willis, and Lucie Fultz. 1991. *Double Stitch: Black Women Write about Mothers and Daughters*. Boston: Beacon Press.

Benjamin, Marina. 1993. "A Question of Identity." In *A Question of Identity: Women, Science, and Literature*, ed. by Marina Benjamin. New Brunswick: Rutgers University Press.

Benmayor, Rina, Ana Juarbe, Celia Alvarez, and Blanca Vázquez. 1987. "For Every Story There Is Another Story Which Stands Before It." In *Stories To Live By: Continuity and Change in Three Generations of Puerto Rican Women*, eds. Rina Benmayor, Ana Juarbe, Celia Alvarez, and Blanca Vázquez. New York: Hunter College of The City University of New York.

Beoku-Betts, Josephine A. 1995. "We Got Our Way of Cooking Things: Women, Food, and Preservation of Cultural Identity among the Gullah." *Gender and Society* 9(5):535–555.

Berch, Bettina. 1980. "Scientific Management in the Home: The Empress's New Clothes." *Journal of American Culture* 3:440–445.

Berk, Sarah Fenstermaker. 1985. *The Gender Factory: The Apportionment of Work in American Households*. New York: Plenum.

Blake, J. Herman. 1977. "'Doctor Can't Do Me No Good': Social Concomitants of Health Care Attitudes and Practices among Elderly Blacks in Isolated Rural Populations." Paper presented at the National Conference of the Black Aged, Washington, D. C.

Bloom, Leslie Rebecca. 1998. *Under the Sign of Hope: Feminist Methodology and Narrative Interpretation*. Albany: State University of New York Press.

Boris, Eileen. 1993. "The Power of Motherhood: Black and White Activist Women Redefine the 'Political'." In *Mothers of a New World: Maternalist Politics and the Origins of Welfare States*, ed. by Seth Koven and Sonya Michel. New York: Routledge.

Bottomley, Gillian. 1992. *From Another Place: Migration and the Politics of Culture*. Cambridge, England: Cambridge University Press.

Brandt, Allan M. 1978. "Racism and Research: The Case of the Tuskegee Syphilis Study." *Hastings Center Report*. 8:21–29.

Brodkin, Karen. 1998. *How Jews Became White Folks and What That Says about Race in America*. New Brunswick: Rutgers University Press.

Brown, Elsa Barkley. 1988. "African-American Women's Quilting: A Framework for Conceptualizing and Teaching African-American Women's History." In *Black Women in America: Social Science Perspectives*, ed. by Michelin R. Malson, Elisabeth Mudimbe-Boyi, Jean F. O'Barr, and Mary Wyer. Chicago: University of Chicago Press.

Brumberg, Joan Jacobs. 1997. *The Body Project: An Intimate History of American Girls*. New York: Random House.

Cameron, Hector Charles. 1921. "Hysteria in the Nursery and in Warfare: A Comparison and a Contrast." *Archives of Pediatrics* 38:193–200.

"Can a Colored Woman Be a Physician?" 1933. *The Crisis* 40(2):33–34.

Carby, Hazel V. 1987. *Reconstructing Womanhood: The Emergence of the Afro-American Woman Novelist*. New York: Oxford University Press.

Carothers, Suzanne. 1990. "Catching Sense: Learning from Our Mothers To Be

Black and Female." In *Uncertain Terms: Negotiating Gender in American Culture*, ed. by Faye Ginsburg and Anna Lowenhaupt Tsing. Boston: Beacon Press.

Carson, Carolyn Leonard. 1994. "And the Results Showed Promise . . . Physicians, Childbirth, and Southern Black Migrant Women, 1916–1930: Pittsburgh as a Case Study." *Journal of American Ethnic History* 14(1):32–64.

Carter, Pam. 1995. *Feminism, Breasts, and Breast-Feeding*. New York: St. Martin's Press.

Chira, Susan. 1994. "Still Guilty After All These Years: A Bouquet of Advice Books for the Working Mom." *New York Times Book Review* 99:11.

Chodorow, Nancy. 1978. *The Reproduction of Mothering: Psychoanalysis and the Sociology of Gender*. Berkeley and Los Angeles: University of California Press.

Clarke, Adele. 1998. *Disciplining Reproduction: Modernity, American Life Sciences, and "The Problem of Sex."* Berkeley and Los Angeles: University of California Press.

Clarke, Adele and Virginia Olesen, eds. 1999. *Revisioning Women, Health, and Healing: Feminist, Cultural, and Technoscience Perspectives*. New York: Routledge.

Clark-Lewis, Elizabeth. 1994. *Living In, Living Out: African American Domestics in Washington, D.C., 1910–1940*. Washington, D.C.: Smithsonian Institution Press.

Code, Lorraine. 1991. *What Can She Know? Feminist Theory and the Construction of Knowledge*. Ithaca: Cornell University Press.

Collins, Patricia Hill. 1990. *Black Feminist Thought: Knowledge, Consciousness, and the Politics of Empowerment*. Boston: Hyman Press.

———. 1998. *Fighting Words: Black Women and the Search for Justice*. Minneapolis: University of Minnesota Press.

———. 1999. "Moving Beyond Gender: Intersectionality and Scientific Knowledge." In *Revisioning Gender*, ed. by Myra Marx Ferree, Judith Lorber, and Beth Hess. Thousand Oaks, Calif.: SAGE Publications.

Collins, Randall. 1992. "Women and the Production of Status Cultures." In *Cultivating Differences: Symbolic Boundaries and the Making of Inequality*, ed. by Michèlle Lamont and Marcel Fournier. Chicago: University of Chicago Press.

Condran, Gretchen A. and Samuel H. Preston. 1994. "Child Mortality Differences, Personal Health Care Practices, and Medical Technology: The United States, 1900–1930." In *Health and Social Change in International Perspective*, ed. by Lincoln C. Chen, Arthur Kleinman, and Norma C. Ware. Boston: Harvard University Press.

Conrad, Peter. 1979. "Types of Medical Social Control." *Sociology of Health and Illness* 1:1–11.

———. 1992. "Medicalization and Social Control." *Annual Review of Sociology* 18:209–232.

Cosslett, Tess. 1994. *Women Writing Childbirth: Modern Discourses of Motherhood*. Manchester, England: Manchester University Press.

Cowan, Neil M. and Ruth Schwartz Cowan. 1989. *Our Parents' Lives: The Americanization of Eastern European Jews*. New York: Basic Books.

Cowan, Ruth Schwartz. 1983. *More Work for Mother: The Ironies of Household Technology from the Open Hearth to the Microwave*. New York: Basic Books.

Cravens, Hamilton. 1985. "Child-Saving in the Age of Professionalism, 1915–1930." In *American Childhood: A Research Guide and Historical Handbook*, ed. by Joseph M. Hawes and N. Ray Hiner. Westport, Conn.: Greenwood.

Dannert, Sylvia G. L. 1966. Dr. Helen Dickens. *Profiles of Negro Womanhood: Twentieth Century*. Vol. 2:91–93. Yonkers, N.Y.: Educational Heritage.

Danzi, Angela D. 1997. *From Home to Hospital: Jewish and Italian American Women and Childbirth, 1920–1940.* New York: University Press of America.

Davies, Carole Boyce. 1985. "Mothering and Healing in Recent Black Women's Fiction." *Sage: A Scholarly Journal on Black Women* 2:41–43.

Davies, Celia. 1988. "The Health Visitor as Mother's Friend: A Woman's Place in Public Health, 1900–1914." *Social History of Medicine* 1:39–59.

Davin, Anna. 1978. "Imperialism and Motherhood." *History Workshop: A Journal of Socialist Historians* 5:9–65.

Davis, Angela. 1981. *Women, Race, and Class.* New York: Vintage Books.

Davis-Floyd, Robbie and Joseph Dumit, eds. 1998. *Cyborg Babies: From Techno-Sex to Techno-Tots.* New York: Routledge.

Deacon, Desley. 1985. "Taylorism in the Home: The Medical Profession, the Infant Welfare Movement, and the Deskilling of Women." *Australian and New Zealand Journal of Sociology* 21:161–173.

DeVault, Marjorie L. 1990. "Talking and Listening from Women's Standpoint: Feminist Strategies for Interviewing and Analysis." *Social Problems* 37:96–116.

———. 1991. *Feeding the Family: The Social Organization of Caring as Gendered Work.* Chicago: University of Chicago Press.

DiLeonardo, Micaela. 1984. *The Varieties of Ethnic Experience: Kinship, Class, and Gender among California Italian-Americans.* Ithaca: Cornell University Press.

Dill, Bonnie Thornton. 1994. *Across the Boundaries of Race and Class: An Exploration of Work and Family among Black Female Domestic Servants.* New York: Garland Publishing.

Donzelot, Jacques. 1979. *The Policing of Families.* New York: Oxford University Press.

Douglas, Mary. 1966. *Purity and Danger: An Analysis of Concepts of Pollution and Taboo.* New York: Praeger.

Edwards, Rosalind. 1990. "Connecting Method and Epistemology: A White Woman Interviewing Black Women." *Women's Studies International Forum* 13:477–490.

Ehrenreich, Barbara and Deirdre English. 1979. *For Her Own Good: 150 Years of the Experts' Advice to Women.* New York: Anchor Press.

Etter-Lewis, Gwendolyn and Michele Foster, eds. 1996. *Unrelated Kin: Race and Gender in Women's Personal Narratives.* New York: Routledge.

Ewen, Elizabeth. 1985. *Immigrant Women in the Land of Dollars: Life and Culture on the Lower East Side, 1890–1925.* New York: Monthly Review Press.

Eyer, Diane. 1993. *Mother-Infant Bonding: A Scientific Fiction.* New Haven: Yale University Press.

Fox, Bonnie J. 1990. "Selling the Mechanized Household: Seventy Years of Ads in *Ladies Home Journal.*" *Gender and Society* 4:25–40.

Frankenberg, Ruth. 1993. *White Women, Race Matters: The Social Construction of Whiteness.* Minneapolis: University of Minnesota Press.

Franklin, Sarah. 1997. *Embodied Progress: A Cultural Account of Assisted Conception.* New York: Routledge.

Franklin, Sarah and Helena Ragoné, eds. 1998. *Reproducing Reproduction: Kinship, Power, and Technological Innovation.* Philadelphia: University of Pennsylvania Press.

Fraser, Gertrude Jacinta. 1998. *African American Midwifery in the South: Dialogues of Birth, Race, and Memory.* Cambridge: Harvard University Press.

Freidson, Eliot. 1970. *Profession of Medicine: A Study of the Sociology of Applied Knowledge.* New York: Harper and Row.

Friedman-Kasaba, Kathie. 1996. *Memories of Migration: Gender, Ethnicity, and Work in the Lives of Jewish and Italian Women in New York, 1870–1924.* Albany: State University of New York Press.

Gans, Herbert J. 1992. Preface. In *Cultivating Differences: Symbolic Boundaries and the Making of Inequality*, ed. by Michèlle Lamont and Marcel Fournier. Chicago: University of Chicago Press.

Gates, Henry Louis, Jr. 1993. "New Negroes, Migration, and Cultural Exchange." In *Jacob Lawrence: The Migration Series*, ed. by Elizabeth Hutton Turner. Washington, D. C.: Rappahannock Press.

Geiger, Susan N. 1986. "Women's Life Histories: Method and Content." *Signs* 11:334–351.

Gengenbach, F. P. 1936. "Medical Routine—From Birth to Adolescence." As Explained by F.P. Gengenbach to Pearl Riggs Crouch. *Hygeia* 14:1080.

Giddings, Paula. 1984. *When and Where I Enter: The Impact of Black Women on Race and Sex in America*. New York: Bantam Books.

Gilligan, Carol. 1982. *In a Different Voice: Psychological Theory and Women's Development*. Cambridge: Harvard University Press.

Glazer, Nona. 1993. *Women's Paid and Unpaid Labor: The Work Transfer in Health Care and Retailing*. Philadelphia: Temple University Press.

Glenn, Evelyn Nakano. 1994. "Social Constructions of Mothering: A Thematic Overview." In *Mothering: Ideology, Experience, and Agency*, ed. by Evelyn Nakano Glenn, Grace Chang, and Linda Rennie Forcey. New York: Routledge.

Glenn, Susan Anita. 1990. *Daughters of the Shtetl: Life and Labor in the Immigrant Generation*. Ithaca: Cornell University Press.

Gluck, Sherna Berger and Daphne Patai, eds. 1991. *Women's Words: The Feminist Practice of Oral History*. New York: Routledge.

Goldberger, Nancy Rule, Jill Mattuck Tarule, Blythe McVicker Clinchy, and Mary Field Belenky, eds. 1996. *Knowledge, Difference, and Power: Essays Inspired by Women's Ways of Knowing*. New York: Basic Books.

Goldstein, Alice, Susan Watkins, and Ann Spector. 1993. "Infant and Childhood Mortality and Health Care among Italians and Jews in the United States, 1910–1940." Paper presented at the annual meetings of the Population Association of America, Cincinnati, Ohio.

Gordon, Linda. 1994. *Pitied but Not Entitled: Single Mothers and the History of Welfare*. New York: Free Press.

Grant, Julia. 1998. *Raising Baby by the Book: The Education of American Mothers*. New Haven: Yale University Press.

Hagood, Margaret Jarman. 1939. *Mothers of the South: Portraiture of the White Tenant Farm Woman*. Chapel Hill: University of North Carolina Press.

Hall, John R. 1992. "The Capital(s) of Cultures: A Nonholistic Approach to Status Situations, Class, Gender, and Ethnicity." In *Cultivating Differences: Symbolic Boundaries and the Making of Inequality*, ed. by Michèlle Lamont and Marcel Fournier. Chicago: University of Chicago Press.

Halpern, Sydney. 1988. *American Pediatrics: The Social Dynamics of Professionalism, 1880–1980*. Berkeley and Los Angeles: University of California Press.

Harding, Sandra. 1986. *The Science Question in Feminism*. Ithaca: Cornell University Press.

————, ed. 1993. *The "Racial" Economy of Science: Toward a Democratic Future*. Bloomington: Indiana University Press.

Harley, Sharon. 1988. "For the Good of Family and Race: Gender, Work, and Domestic Roles in the Black Community, 1880–1930." In *Black Women in America: Social Science Perspectives*, ed. by Micheline R. Malson, Elisabeth Mudimbe-Boyi, Jean F. O'Barr, and Mary Wyer. Chicago: University of Chicago Press.

Hays, Sharon. 1996. *The Cultural Contradictions of Motherhood*. New Haven: Yale University Press.

Heinze, Andrew R. 1990. *Adapting to Abundance: Jewish Immigrants, Mass Consumption, and the Search for American Identity*. New York: Columbia University Press.

Hershberg, Theodore, Alan N. Burstein, Eugene P. Ericksen, Stephanie Greenberg, and William L. Yancey. 1979. "A Tale of Three Cities: Blacks and Immigrants in Philadelphia: 1850–1880, 1930 and 1970. *The Annals of The American Academy of Political and Social Science* 441:55–81.

Higginbotham, Evelyn Brooks. 1993. *Righteous Discontent: The Women's Movement in the Black Baptist Church, 1880–1920*. Cambridge: Harvard University Press.

Hine, Darlene Clark. 1996. "Black Migration to the Urban Midwest: The Gender Dimension, 1915–1945." In *The New African American Urban History*, ed. by Kenneth W. Goings and Raymond A. Mohl. Thousand Oaks, Calif.: SAGE Publications.

Hobbs, Margaret. 1988. "'A Kitchen That Wastes No Steps . . .': Gender, Class and the Home Improvement Plan, 1936–1940." *Social History* 21:9–37.

Holt, Marilyn. 1995. *Linoleum, Better Babies, and the Modern Farm Woman, 1890–1930*. Albuquerque: University of New Mexico Press.

hooks, bell. 1990. *Yearning: Race, Gender, and Cultural Politics*. Boston: South End Press.

Huenekens, E. J. 1925. "The Preschool Child with Especial Reference to Its Emotional Life and Habit Problems." *American Medical Association Section on Diseases of Children* 76:17–27.

Humphries, Drew. 1999. *Crack Mothers: Pregnancy, Drugs, and the Media*. Columbus: Ohio State University Press.

Hyman, Paula. 1994. "Feminist Studies and Modern Jewish History." In *Feminist Perspectives on Jewish Studies*, ed. by Lynn Davidman and Shelly Tenenbaum. New Haven: Yale University Press.

Isaacs, Miriam. 1941. *What Every Jewish Woman Should Know: A Guide for Jewish Women*. New York: The Jewish Book Club.

Joeres, Ruth-Ellen Boetcher and Barbara Laslett. 1993. "Personal Narratives: A Selection of Recent Works." *Signs* 18:389–391.

Jones, Jacqueline. 1985. *Labor of Love, Labor of Sorrow: Black Women, Work, and the Family, From Slavery to the Present*. New York: Random House.

Jones, Kathleen W. 1983. "Sentiment and Science: The Late Nineteenth-Century Pediatrician as Mother's Advisor." *Journal of Social History* 17:79–96.

Joselit, Jenna Weissman. 1994. *The Wonders of America: Reinventing Jewish Culture, 1880–1950*. New York: Hill and Wang.

Kaplan, E. Ann. 1994. "Look Who's Talking, Indeed: Fetal Images in Recent North American Visual Culture." In *Mothering: Ideology, Experience, and Agency*, ed. by Evelyn Nakano Glenn, Grace Chang, and Linda Rennie Forcey. New York: Routledge.

Kerber, Linda. 1995. "A Constitutional Right To Be Treated Like American Ladies: Women and the Obligations of Citizenship." In *U.S. History as Women's History: New Feminist Essays*, eds. Linda Kerber, Alice Kessler-Harris, and Kathryn Kish Sklar. Chapel Hill: University of North Carolina Press.

King, Deborah K. 1988. "Multiple Jeopardy, Multiple Consciousness: The Context of a Black Feminist Ideology." In *Black Women in America: Social Science Perspectives*, ed. by Micheline R. Malson, Elisabeth Mudimbe-Boyi, Jean F. O'Barr, and Mary Wyer. Chicago: University of Chicago Press.

Kraut, Alan M. 1994. *Silent Travelers: Germs, Genes, and the "Immigrant Menace"*. New York: Basic Books.

Kuznick, Peter J. 1994. "Losing the World of Tomorrow: The Battle over the Presentation of Science at the 1939 World's Fair." *American Quarterly* 46:341–373.

Ladd-Taylor, Molly. 1986. *Raising a Baby the Government Way: Mothers' Letters to the Children's Bureau, 1915–1932.* New Brunswick: Rutgers University Press.

———. 1994. *Mother-Work: Women, Child Welfare, and the State, 1890–1930.* Chicago: University of Illinois Press.

Ladd-Taylor, Molly and Lauri Umansky, eds. 1998. *"Bad" Mothers: The Politics of Blame in Twentieth-Century America.* New York: New York University Press.

LaFollette, Marcel C. 1990. *Making Science Our Own: Public Images of Science, 1910–1955.* Chicago: University of Chicago Press.

Lamont, Michèlle and Marcel Fournier, eds. 1992. *Cultivating Differences: Symbolic Boundaries and the Making of Inequality.* Chicago: University of Chicago Press.

Lamphere, Louise. 1993. *Sunbelt Working Mothers: Reconciling Family and Factory.* Ithaca: Cornell University Press.

Lazarre, Jane. 1996. *Beyond the Whiteness of Whiteness: Memoir of a White Mother of Black Sons.* Durham, N.C.: Duke University Press.

Leavitt, Judith. 1986. *Brought to Bed: Child-Bearing in America, 1750–1950.* New York: Oxford University Press.

Lee, Valerie. 1996. *Granny Midwives and Black Women Writers: Double-Dutched Readings.* New York: Routledge.

Lemke-Santangelo, Gretchen. 1996. *Abiding Courage: African American Migrant Women and the East Bay Community.* Chapel Hill: The University of North Carolina Press.

Lewis, Earl. 1996. "Connecting Memory, Self, and the Power of Place in African American Urban History." In *The New African American Urban History,* ed. by Kenneth W. Goings and Raymond A. Mohl. Thousand Oaks, Calif.: SAGE Publications.

Litt, Jacquelyn. 1990. "Are We (Still) Medical Sociologists?" *Medical Sociology Newsletter.* Summer.

———. 1993. "Pediatrics and the Development of Middle-Class Motherhood." *Research in the Sociology of Health Care* 10:161–173.

———. 1996. "Mothering, Medicalization, and Jewish Identity, 1928–1940." *Gender and Society* 10:185–198.

———. 1997. "American Medicine and Divided Motherhood: Views from the Lives of Jewish and African American Women." *The Sociological Quarterly* 38:285–302.

———. 1999. "Managing the Street, Isolating the Household: African American Mothers Respond to Neighborhood Deterioration." *Race, Gender, and Class* 6:90–108.

Litt, Jacquelyn and Maureen McNeil. 1997. "Biological Markers and Social Differentiation: *Crack Babies* and the Construction of the Dangerous Mother." *Health Care for Women International* 18:31–41.

Logan, Onnie Lee. 1989. *Motherwit: An Alabama Midwife's Story.* New York: E. P. Dutton.

McBride, David. 1989. *Integrating the City of Medicine: Blacks in Philadelphia Health Care, 1910–1965.* Philadelphia: Temple University Press.

McClary, Andrew. 1980. "Germs Are Everywhere: The Germ Threat as Seen in Magazine Articles." *Journal of American Culture* 3:33–46.

McMahon, Martha. 1995. *Engendering Motherhood: Identity and Self-Transformation in Women's Lives.* New York: Guilford Press.

McNeil Consumer Products Company. 1999. "McNeil Consumer Healthcare: Corporate History." Fort Washington, Penn.

McNeil, Maureen. 1988. "Newton as National Hero." In *Let Newton Be! A New Perspective on His Life and Works*, ed. by John Fauvel, Raymond Flood, Michael Shortland, and Robin Wilson. New York: Oxford University Press.

McRobbie, Angela. 1982. "The Politics of Feminist Research: Between Talk, Text, and Action." *Feminist Review* 12:46–57.

Marchland, Roland. 1985. *Advertising the American Dream: Making Way for Modernity, 1920–1940*. Berkeley and Los Angeles: University of California Press.

Marcus, Joseph H. 1925. "Negativism in Childhood." *Archives of Pediatrics* 42:455–461.

Markens, Susan, Carole H. Browner, and Nancy Press. 1997. "Feeding the Fetus: On Interrogating the Notion of Maternal-Fetal Conflict." *Feminist Studies* 23(2):351–372.

Marks, Carole. 1989. *Farewell—We're Good and Gone: The Great Black Migration*. Bloomington: Indiana University Press.

Martin, Emily. 1992. *The Woman in the Body: A Cultural Analysis of Reproduction*. 2d ed. Boston: Beacon Press.

———. 1994a. *Flexible Bodies: Tracking Immunity in American Culture from the Days of Polio to the Age of AIDS*. Boston: Beacon Press.

———. 1994b. "Anthropology and the Cultural Study of Science: Citadels, Rhizomes, and String Figures." Keynote address to the Society for Social Studies of Science, New Orleans.

Mechling, Jay. 1975. "Advice to Historians on Advice to Mothers." *Journal of Social History* 9:44–63.

Meckel, Richard A. 1990. *Save the Babies: American Public Health Reform and the Prevention of Infant Mortality, 1850–1929*. Baltimore: Johns Hopkins University Press.

Merchant, Carolyn. 1980. *The Death of Nature: Women, Ecology, and the Scientific Revolution*. New York: Harper and Row.

Meyers, Garry C. 1929. "Problems of the Pediatrician as the Psychologist Sees Them." *American Journal of Diseases of Children* 38:676.

Miles, R. S. 1921. "Common Nervous Conditions of Children." *Archives of Pediatrics* 38: 664–671.

Mink, Gwendolyn. 1995. *The Wages of Motherhood: Inequality in the Welfare State, 1917–1942*. Ithaca: Cornell University Press.

Moore, Deborah Dash. 1981. *At Home in America: Second Generation New York Jews*. New York: Columbia University Press.

Mullings, Leigh. 1997. *On Our Own Terms: Race, Class, and Gender in the Lives of African American Women*. New York: Routledge.

Newman, Louise Michele. 1985. *Men's Ideas/Women's Realities: Popular Science, 1870–1915*. New York: Pergamon Press.

Oakley, Ann. 1981. "Interviewing Women: A Contradiction in Terms." In *Doing Feminist Research*, ed. by Helen Roberts. London: Routledge and Kegan Paul.

———. 1984. *The Captured Womb: A History of the Medical Care of Pregnant Women*. New York: Basil Blackwell.

Omi, Michael and Howard Winant. 1994. *Racial Formation in the United States from the 1960s to the 1990s*. 2d ed. New York: Routledge and Kegan Paul.

Palmer, Phyllis. 1989. *Domesticity and Dirt: Housewives and Domestic Servants in the United States, 1920–1945*. Philadelphia: Temple University Press.

Peiss, Kathy. 1998. *Hope in a Jar: The Making of America's Beauty Culture.* New York: Metropolitan Books.

Pescosolido, Bernice A. 1992. "Beyond Rational Choice: The Social Dynamics of How People Seek Help." *American Journal of Sociology* 97:1096–1138.

Petchesky, Rosalind. 1990. *Abortion and Women's Choice: The State, Sexuality, and Reproductive Freedom.* Boston: Northeastern University Press.

Phillips, Kimberley L. 1996. "'But It Is a Fine Place to Make Money': Migration and African-American Families in Cleveland, 1915–1929." *Journal of Social History* 30:393–413.

Polakow, Valerie. 1993. *Lives on the Edge: Single Mothers and Their Children in the Other America.* Chicago: University of Chicago Press.

Porter, Roy. 1985. "The Patient's View: Doing Medical History from Below." *Theory and Society* 14:175–198.

Rapp, Rayna. 1990. "Constructing Amniocentesis: Maternal and Medical Discourses." In *Uncertain Terms: Negotiating Gender in American Culture,* ed. by Faye Ginsburg and Anna Lowenhaupt Tsing. Boston: Beacon Press.

———. 1999. "One New Reproductive Technology, Multiple Sites: How Feminist Methodology Bleeds into Everyday Life." In Adele C. Clarke and Virginia L. Olesen, eds. *Revisioning Women, Health, and Healing: Feminist, Cultural, and Technoscience Perspectives.* New York: Routledge.

Reinharz, Shulamit. 1992. *Feminist Methods in Social Research.* New York: Oxford University Press.

Reissman, Catherine K. 1987. "When Gender Is Not Enough: Women Interviewing Women." *Gender and Society* 1:172–207.

———. 1989. "Women and Medicalization: A New Perspective." In *Perspectives in Medical Sociology,* ed. by Phil Brown. Belmont, Calif.: Wadsworth.

Rich, Adrienne. 1976. *Of Woman Born: Motherhood as Experience and Institution.* New York: W. W. Norton.

Rollins, Judith. 1985. *Between Women: Domestics and Their Employers.* Philadelphia: Temple University Press.

Rose, Elizabeth. 1994. "From Sponge Cake to *Hamentashen*: Jewish Identity in a Jewish Settlement House, 1885–1952." *Journal of Ethnic History* 13:3–23.

Rosen, Philip. 1983. "German Jews vs. Russian Jews in Philadelphia Philanthropy." In *Jewish Life in Philadelphia 1830–1940,* ed. by Murray Friedman. Philadelphia: ISHI Publications.

Rosenwald, George C. and Richard L. Ochberg, eds. 1992. *Storied Lives: The Cultural Politics of Self-Understanding.* New Haven: Yale University Press.

Rothman, Barbara Katz. 1986. *The Tentative Pregnancy: Prenatal Diagnosis and the Future of Motherhood.* New York: Viking Press.

———. 1989. *Recreating Motherhood: Ideology and Technology in a Patriarchal Society.* New York: W. W. Norton.

———. 1998. *Genetic Maps and Human Imaginations: The Limits of Science in Understanding Who We Are.* New York: W. W. Norton.

Rothman, Sheila. 1978. *Women's Proper Place: A History of Changing Ideals and Practices, 1970 to the Present.* New York: Basic Books.

Rubin, Joan Shelley. 1983. "Information Please: Culture and Expertise in the Interwar Period." *American Quarterly* 35:499–517.

Ruddick, Sara. 1982. "Maternal Thinking." In *Rethinking the Family: Some Feminist Questions,* ed. by Barrie Thorne and Marilyn Yalom. New York: Longman.

Rydell, Robert W. 1993. *World of Fairs: The Century-of-Progress Expositions.* Chicago: University of Chicago Press.

Scheper-Hughes, Nancy. 1992. *Death without Weeping: The Violence of Everyday Life in Brazil*. Berkeley and Los Angeles: University of California Press.

Schlossman, Steven L. 1976. "Before Home Start: Notes toward a History of Parent Education in America, 1897–1929." *Harvard Educational Review* 46(3):436–467.

Shapiro, Laura. 1986. *Perfection Salad: Women and Cooking at the Turn of the Century*. New York: Farrar, Straus, and Giroux.

Shopes, Linda. 1994. "When Women Interview Women—and Then Publish It: Reflections on Oral History, Women's History, and Public History." *Journal of Women's History* 6:98–108.

Sidel, Ruth. 1986. *Women and Children Last: The Plight of Poor Women in Affluent America*. New York: Viking Press.

Simonds, Wendy. 1992. *Women and Self-Help Culture: Reading between the Lines*. New Brunswick: Rutgers University Press.

Sklar, Kathryn Kish. 1973. *Catharine Beecher: A Study in American Domesticity*. New Haven: Yale University Press.

Smith, Dorothy E. 1984. "Textually Mediated Social Organization." *The International Social Science Journal* 36:59–75.

———. 1987. *The Everyday World as Problematic: A Feminist Sociology*. Boston: Northeastern University Press.

———. 1989. "Women's Work as Mothers: A New Look at the Relation of Class, Family and Social Achievement." *Perspectives on Social Problems* 1:109–125.

———. 1990. *Texts, Facts, and Femininity: Exploring the Relations of Ruling*. New York: Routledge.

Smith, Dorothy E. and Alison J. Griffith. 1990. "Coordinating the Uncoordinated: Mothering, Schooling, and the Family Wage." *Perspectives on Social Problems*. 2:25–45.

Smith, Sidonie. 1993. "Who's Talking/Who's Talking Back? The Subject of Personal Narrative." *Signs* 18:392–407.

Smith, Susan L. 1995. *Sick and Tired of Being Sick and Tired: Black Women's Health Activism in America, 1890–1950*. Philadelphia: University of Pennsylvania Press.

Snow, Loudell F. 1993. *Walkin' over Medicine*. Boulder: Westview Press.

Spock, Benjamin M. 1946. *The Pocket Book of Baby and Child Care*. New York: Pocket Books.

Spock, Benjamin and Mary Morgan. 1989. *Spock on Spock: A Memoir of Growing Up with the Century*. New York: Pantheon Books.

Stacey, Judith. 1994. "Imagining Feminist Ethnography: A Response to Elizabeth E. Wheatley." *Women's Studies International Forum* 17:417–419.

Stack, Carol. 1974. *All Our Kin: Strategies for Survival in a Black Community*. New York: Harper and Row.

———. 1996. *Call to Home: African Americans Reclaim the Rural South*. New York: Harper and Row.

Stage, Sarah and Virginia Vincenti, eds. 1997. *Rethinking Home Economics: Women and the Story of a Profession*. Ithaca: Cornell University Press.

Starr, Paul. 1982. *The Social Transformation of American Medicine*. New York: Basic Books.

Stivers, Camilla. 1993. "Reflections on the Role of Personal Narrative in Social Science." *Signs* 18:408–425.

Strathern, Marilyn. 1992. *Reproducing the Future: Essays on Anthropology, Kinship, and the New Reproductive Technologies*. New York: Routledge.

Tabak, Robert Phillip. 1990. *The Transformation of Jewish Identity: The Philadelphia Experience, 1919–1945*. Ann Arbor, Mich.: University Microfilms.

Theriot, Nancy M. 1993. "Women's Voices in Nineteenth-Century Medical Discourse: A Step Toward Deconstructing Science." *Signs* 19:1–31.

Tomes, Nancy J. 1997. "Spreading the Germ Theory: Sanitary Science, Household Bacteriology, and the Home Economics Movement, 1880–1930." In *Rethinking Home Economics: Women and the Story of a Profession*, ed. by Sarah Stage and Virginia Vincenti. Ithaca: Cornell University Press.

Toth, Emily. 1989. "Sharing Stories, Sharing Lives." *Women's Review of Books* 7:21.

Tsing, Anna Lowenhaupt. 1990. "Monster Stories: Women Charged with Perinatal Endangerment." In *Uncertain Terms: Negotiating Gender in American Culture*, ed. by Faye Ginsburg and Anna Lowenhaupt Tsing. Boston: Beacon Press.

Umansky, Lauri. 1996. *Motherhood Reconceived: Feminism and the Legacies of the Sixties*. New York: New York University Press.

Vrettos, Athena. 1989. "Curative Domains: Women, Healing, and History in Black Women's Narratives." *Women's Studies* 16:455–473.

Walkerdine, Valerie and Helen Lucey. 1989. *Democracy in the Kitchen: Regulating Mothers and Socializing Daughters*. London: Virago Press.

Walzer, Susan. 1998. *Thinking about the Baby: Gender and Transitions into Parenthood*. Philadelphia: Temple University Press.

Ware, Susan. 1982. *Holding Their Own: American Women in the 1930s*. Boston: Twayne Publishers.

Watkins, Susan Cotts and Angela Danzi. 1995. "Women's Gossip and Social Change: Childbirth and Fertility Control among Italian and Jewish Women in the United States, 1920–1940." *Gender and Society* 9:469–490.

Weinberg, Sidney Stahl. 1988. *The World of Our Mothers: The Lives of Jewish Immigrant Women*. Chapel Hill: University of North Carolina Press.

Weiss, Nancy Pottishman. 1977. "Mother, the Invention of Necessity." *American Quarterly* 29:519–546.

———. 1978. "The Mother-Child Dyad: Perceptions of Mothers and Children in Twentieth-Century Child-Rearing Manuals." *Journal of Social Issues* 34:29–45.

Wheatley, Elizabeth E. 1994a. "Dances with Feminists: Truths, Dares, and Ethnographic Stares." *Women's Studies International Forum* 17:421–423.

———. 1994b. "How Can We Engender Ethnography with a Feminist Imagination?" *Women's Studies International Forum* 17:403–416.

White, Deborah Gray. 1985. *Ar'n't I a Woman? Female Slaves in the Plantation South*. New York: W. W. Norton.

Whiteman, Maxwell. 1973. "Philadelphia's Jewish Neighborhoods." In *The Peoples of Philadelphia: A History of Ethnic Groups and Lower-Class Life, 1790–1940*, ed. by Allen F. Davis and Mark H. Haller. Philadelphia: Temple University Press.

Yans-McLaughlin, Virginia. 1990. "Metaphors of Self in History: Subjectivity, Oral Narrative, and Immigration Studies." In *Immigration Considered*, ed. by Virginia Yans-McLaughlin. New York: Oxford University Press.

Young, Iris Marion. 1990. "The Ideal of Community and the Politics of Difference." In *Feminism/Postmodernism*, ed. by Linda J. Nicholson. New York: Routledge.

Zaretsky, Eli. 1976. *Capitalism, the Family, and Personal Life*. New York: Harper and Row.

Zelizer, Viviana A. 1985. *Pricing the Priceless Child: The Changing Social Value of Children*. New York: Basic Books.

Zola, Irving Kenneth. 1994. "Medicine as an Institution of Social Control." In *The*

Sociology of Health and Illness: Critical Perspectives, ed. by Peter Conrad and Rochelle Kern. New York: St. Martin's Press.

Zuckerman, Michael. 1975. "Dr. Spock: The Confidence Man." In *The Family in History,* ed. by Charles E. Rosenberg. Philadelphia: University of Pennsylvania Press.

Index

About the Author

Jacquelyn S. Litt got her B.A. from William Smith College and her Ph.D. in Sociology from the University of Pennsylvania. She is currently an assistant professor in sociology and women's studies at Iowa State University, and won the Early Excellence in Teaching Award in 1999 from its College of Liberal Arts and Science . Her recent publications include articles in *Gender and Society*, *The Sociological Quarterly*, *Health Care for Women International*, and *Race, Gender, and Class*. She is now researching how low-income mothers are managing issues of privacy and care work in the context of U.S. welfare reform.